On Eagles' Wings

On Eagles' Wings

Sara Eggleston

Healthy Life Press
Orlando, Florida

ON EAGLES' WINGS

Copyright © 2011, 2013 by Sara Eggleston

Published by:
Healthy Life Press, 2603 Drake Drive, Orlando, FL 32810
www.healthylifepress.com

Cover design by: Adrian Vergin and Judy Johnson
Cover photo by: David B. Biebel

Printed in the United States of America

Library of Congress Cataloging-in-Publication Data
Eggleston, Sara
  On Eagles' Wings

ISBN 978-1-939267-24-5

1. Autobiography; 2. Christian Living; 3. Self-help

Dedication

I dedicate this book to my mom and dad, who gave me life – physical, emotional, and spiritual – and who were the best of parents.

Acknowledgements

I wish to acknowledge the encouragement and support of my colleagues Kathrine Lee and Jeff Olson, and my wonderful husband, Frank, who has given me every- thing that I could ever want. He is the best of husbands, my support, my best friend, my lover, my spiritual leader, and the best dad and granddad. I feel so blessed and fortunate to be his wife. We believe that God put us together. We thank God every day for each other and for our life on this earth. We pray that God will use us to help others.

About the Cover:

The cover photo was taken March 16, 2009 by Dave Biebel, my publisher, who was at the time fishing with his dad on the Sebastian River, in Sebastian, Florida. When his dad mentioned that the cloud with the sun setting behind it looked like an eagle, Dave grabbed his digital camera and snapped this remarkable photo. Prints are available for purchase, in various sizes. See the back pages of this book for ordering information or visit: www.healthylifepress.com, and click "Poster" on the main page menu.

Foreword

The purpose of this book is to give hope to anyone facing adversity, that out of the ashes of their life God can truly take them to the highest point . . . the zenith of His existence. For He, and only He, CAN raise a phoenix from the ashes of despair and desperation.

As the apostle Paul wrote in Ephesians 3:20-21: "Now unto him that is able to do exceeding abundantly above all that we ask or think, according to the power that worketh in us, unto him be glory in the church by Christ Jesus throughout all ages, world without end. Amen."

We just need to ask for His help. And when we do, we have this promise, from which the book's title comes: ". . . they that wait upon the Lord shall renew their strength; they shall mount up with wings as eagles; they shall run and not be weary; they shall walk and not faint" (Isaiah 40:31).

I have written this text as a "stream of consciousness," in that when I've just described something that happened, and my mind connected that with something or someone else of importance in my long journey from my idyllic childhood, through chaos, to real joy, I wrote about that recollection next. And instead of interrupting this stream of consciousness with a lot of "lessons learned," I put some of the lessons I've learned along the way in the Appendix at the back of the book, where I hope that you will find them helpful.

All the stories in this book are true, but in most cases the identities of individuals involved have been disguised in order to protect their privacy.

7

Sara Eggleston

TABLE OF CONTENTS

DEDICATION   5

ACKNOWLEDGEMENTS   6

FOREWORD   7

PART I: LIVING THE SIMPLE LIFE

CHAPTER 1: JUST AN ORDINARY FARM GIRL   13

CHAPTER 2: FRUGALITY, FUN, AND FRITO LAY   27

PART II: LIVING IN FEAR

CHAPTER 3: BLIND LOVE, BOUNCED CHECKS,
AND BAD COMPANY   41

CHAPTER 4: A REIGN OF TERROR   57

PART III: LIVING BY FAITH

CHAPTER 5: A BOLD SPIRIT   79

CHAPTER 6: KEEPSAKES, COPIERS, AND THE TEACHING MOMENT   95

PART IV: LIVING IN VICTORY

CHAPTER 7: MARRIED TO THE DENTIST OF THE WORLD,
SERVING THE CREATOR OF THE WORLD   113

APPENDIX:

LESSONS LEARNED ON THE JOURNEY   127

HEALTHY LIFE PRESS RESOURCES   142

Sara Eggleston

Part I

Living The Simple Life

Sara Eggleston

CHAPTER 1

Just an Ordinary Farm Girl

Growing up on the farm in the small town of Munday, Texas, with three brothers and several boy cousins living close by was a simple life. We had a key to the church and a key to the school and were there for every event whenever the doors opened. My mom taught us the Bible while she cooked, strained milk, churned butter, made bread, canned vegetables, sewed our clothes, cleaned house, washed and ironed, and washed dishes. She taught me to do the same chores.

Dad went out the door at the crack of dawn every morning to milk cows and tend to livestock before he started his farm work. I often barreled out of bed to go with Dad since he was my idol. On Sunday, the schedule was different. We all went to church together.

When I was maybe three or four years old, my dad and uncle were going to visit my Great-Grandpa Offutt, who lived in Glen Rose, Texas. Great-Grandpa was in his last days. He lived close to where my father had been born in Glen Rose, on the Seven Knobs, with Uncle Cy, my bachelor uncle, in this old-looking brown house where my cousin Peggy taught me to do string games.

The only way Daddy would let me go was if I would promise not to say a word, and especially not to ask every five minutes or so, "How much farther is it, Daddy?"

Daddy told me, "Sissy, you can go with us if you won't talk. You have to be still. I want to talk with your uncle, without being interrupted. Can you do that?"

Considering my exuberant nature, it was very hard for me to keep that requirement, but I did.

Every Christmas or Thanksgiving we went to see my grandmother on my daddy's side, out in Patricia – a very small town out on the plains. We would have turkey and dressing and her special fruit salad that we still make today – and we would have so much fun, farm family fun. On Thanksgiving, Texas A&M always played Texas, so I would get dressed up in my little cheerleader's skirt and root for one school or the other. I think I probably knew the Aggie War Hymn by the time I was five. It starts like this:

"Hullabaloo, Caneck, Caneck! Hullabaloo, Caneck, Caneck! All hail to dear old Texas A&M; Rally around Maroon and White; Good luck to dear old Texas Aggies; They are the boys who show the real old fight; That good old Aggie Spirit thrills us; And makes us yell and yell and yell! So let's fight for dear old Texas A&M; We're gonna beat you all to h— Chigaroogarem, Chigaroogarem."

In the summertime I would also go see my grandmother. She did not have indoor plumbing, so I remember going out to the outhouse and being afraid that I was going to sit on a snake or something. I was so scared. When I was little, maybe three, I rode the bus with my brother George, and Grandmother made me sleep by myself. I remember sniveling and crying and then George came and crawled under the covers and held my hand and said, "Sissy, don't cry, I'm here. I'll take care of you." George was my hero.

Sometimes we would go over to my aunt's in Seminole. Our uncle was a photographer. When I was four he took our pictures and enlarged them into life-sized photos of my brother and me and put them in the window of his studio. When my mom and dad came to pick us up, our pictures were there, and my parents at first thought that we were standing in the window, because they were so lifelike. My aunt had fixed my hair for that picture, and I remember thinking how pretty I looked. I didn't usually think I was pretty at all, but I thought I looked pretty that day because she had fixed my hair.

I wanted to learn to swim, but my dad had a real fear of water and would not allow me, so even today I still do not swim that well, even though I've had lessons. He was afraid for me to get in the water. He said, "You can't get in the water until you learn to swim." Of course that's a problem since you have to get into the water to learn to swim in the first place, like you have to get on the bicycle to learn how to ride the bicycle.

School was always very important to me. When my brother George was in first grade and I was three, his teacher got sick and had to have surgery. My mom was the only certified teacher in our small town, so the superintendent asked her to take George's class for six weeks. Mom agreed if I could come, too. The superintendent said I could come if I could be quiet – everybody already knew about my exuberant nature. During that six-week period, I learned to read along with the other first graders as my mom taught the children from the Scott Foresman series with Dick, Jane, Sally, Spot, and Puff.

I was taught God's values and given a strong work ethic on the farm. I wanted to be the best I could be, but sometimes it was hard to control my exuberance. For example, when I was four years old Dad told us that Mom was going to have another baby. He asked my older brother George and me to not tell anyone. George and I went to the Beck farm later in the day, and I was so excited that I could not resist telling Mrs. Beck. My dad was very disappointed in me and washed my mouth out with soap when we got home. So I was exposed early to the value of keeping a confidence. Although I was only four years old, a lot was expected of both George and me, even then.

The baby Mom was expecting, Dan, turned out to be a real Daddy's boy. He would cry to go with Dad, and he made life miserable for Mom at home when Dad was gone. Dan was a rambunctious toddler. One day when Mom needed to sew a costume for George to be in a play at school, and Dan was still very young, Mom tied him to the leg of her sewing machine with cup towels knotted together so she could keep an eye on him. Mom could not trust Dan out of her sight for even a minute. He climbed like a monkey and was everywhere at once. Dan later used this great energy to his advantage in sports, for he was an outstanding athlete. But when Dad came in that day and saw what Mom had done, he immediately took Dan with him.

Throughout my entire childhood and adolescence, we lived in the house where I had been born. Before Dan came along, George and I once went up into the front bedroom looking for Christmas toys. We found them up in the top of the closet, and we were so excited, we pushed the sewing machine over into the closet, and George stood on that and hoisted me up so I could reach them. We brought them all down and went through them, then put them all back carefully. Then we pushed the sewing machine carefully back into place. When we went into the kitchen where my mom and dad both were – for some reason that day Dad wasn't out on the tractor, maybe because it was the dead of winter – I asked, "Mom, is there really a Santa Claus?" She looked over at my dad – I can still remember the look she gave him – because we'd been gone a long time and we'd been quiet for a long time. Then she said, "Well, you know, the spirit of Santa Claus is very important. And Santa has lots of helpers. In fact, Santa Claus can have helpers just about anywhere we look!" Then she added, "Those who believe in the spirit of Christmas and the spirit of giving always get presents, but those who don't believe don't get any presents." I always have believed.

So George and I looked at each other wondering if we should say anything else, and of course they saw our guilty looks, and Mother said, "Did you find something in the front bedroom that I need to know about?"

Of course we thought she knew everything, so we confessed . . . and then she gave us our presents early, which wasn't any fun at all. So when the little brothers came along we decided that we should keep the spirit of Christmas and the spirit of giving and the spirit of Santa Claus alive, and we all pretended that there was a Santa Claus and that he just had helpers. So that was a great lesson to me.

When I was a young child, I rebelled against my mom. I just didn't want to do what she wanted me to do. It didn't make any difference what it was. If I was to sweep the floor, I would drag the broom down the middle of the floor. She would come in and see that it hadn't been done right and she would make me do it over. If she told me something was black, I would say it was white. I argued with her constantly.

When I cooked, I would mess up every pan in the house – it would be the biggest mess. Mom was a very neat, precise person, so I had to make the biggest mess just to hear her fuss at me. Then, of course, I had to clean it up. But that didn't matter to me. The main thing for me was the kick I got out of upsetting her, and I would do whatever I could do to achieve that. It was fun, like a game to me. When I was really bad, she would set me in the corner, knowing that if she sent me to my room, it wouldn't be any kind of punishment because I would just read, and I loved to read. So she would make me sit in the corner on the stool in the dark. To get back at her, I peeled all the wallpaper off the wall in the corner. Of course that got me in more trouble, but I had to have something to do. I was always in motion – and that's still a part of who I am.

It was so bad that once she said to my dad, "I can't raise her. I can't raise her. She's too strong-willed." And my dad said, "She can lead the whole town to heaven or lead them to hell, but you cannot give up on her. I've got three boys to raise. Do not raise your hand off of her."

And Mom's the reason I learned to channel that energy. I give her the credit truly – there's no animosity at all – for anything that was ever done. She was a wonderful mother to all of us. We all revere her for what she did and who she was. She was a real mother for all of us. Everywhere we went, she took us. She was a part of everything we did. All she ever wanted to do was be a mom and raise her children. And Daddy gave her the money to do that, so she didn't have to work outside the home. She'd been a teacher before she married Dad, but she didn't have to do that anymore after they married.

When I was in second grade, my older brother and I got our own small bank accounts so we could learn to take care of our money. I thought as long as I had checks, I had money, so it was not long until I was overdrawn at the bank. Daddy said he had gotten a notice from Mr. Brawley, the bank president, that I'd overdrawn my bank account. "Well, I couldn't have," I said. "I still have checks."

"No, no, no," Daddy replied. "You've spent more than you've got. You've got to go tell Mr. Brawley that you're sorry and give him some money."

"You'll do that for me, won't you?" I asked.

"Oh, no," he said. "I won't. You'll do that yourself. I will take you and go with you, but you have to go in and tell him that you're sorry."

I'll never forget sitting in that big leather chair in the Munday First National Bank with Mr. Brawley – I loved both him and his wife very much. They didn't have any children. I thought he was quite stern. He smiled gently at me, because he realized that I didn't understand what happened in a checkbook. I told him I was sorry, thanked him for teaching me, and gave him some money. On the way home in the pickup truck, my dad said, "Well, Sissy, I guess I didn't explain that to you very well, did I? I'm really sorry." And that's how I learned that great people say they're sorry when they've made a mistake.

I wanted to have perfect attendance in school and did until I was in third grade when I caught the mumps from my brother George. I tried to hide the fact that I had them and even went sick to a basketball game with my parents. I vividly remember wearing a sweater with a high neck and trying to sit at the game out of my all-knowing mother's eyes. She caught me, of course, and I missed school for awhile until I got better.

My ability to keep a confidence was tested again that year. Often things come back to haunt us until we learn the lesson. A shy girl named Susan, who was an only child, admired me and shared with me on the playground that she had torn her panties on the slide. Being a great tomboy and often tearing my clothes, I was totally insensitive to her feelings. I thought it was funny that such a precious, perfect little girl did one time what I always seemed to do. I lay down on the playground and started laughing. All the other children gathered round, and I laughingly told them that Susan had torn her panties. That afternoon when I got off the bus to run into our home, my mom and dad were waiting for me. They told me that Susan's mother had killed herself that day and that we were going to comfort the family. We went to her home where Susan was with her father and grandmother. Susan refused to speak to me. I always believed that it was because I had laughed at her, though I hadn't meant any harm. I was devastated and so sorry for my actions that I vowed to try to never hurt anyone again.

Later that year I was diagnosed with a hyperactive, toxic goiter. We discovered my illness in Hot Springs, Arkansas, on an infrequent family vacation. The weather was scorching hot as we walked to the hot springs. I could not keep up, and Dad yelled at me. This reprimand was most unusual since I was the apple of his eye, and he usually had only to look at me for me to straighten up. My heart was racing so fast, probably over two hundred beats a minute, and I almost passed out. My throat was also growing closed. I was the youngest child to have this type of disease and made medical history for a few months until they found another child in South America who was even younger with the same problem. I loved being famous for a few months.

I was only allowed to go to school in the mornings in grade four. I rested in the afternoons. I had to stay in bed all day during that summer before having successful surgery at Baylor Hospital in Dallas. It was during this time that I learned that my mom really loved me. Until this time, my very reserved mother had never said the words "I love you" out loud to me. Mom lived it rather than spoke it, but I longed to hear the words. Mom read aloud to me when she came to visit to help keep me calm.

One day during my illness, I heard my mom crying, and I promised God that I would be a good little girl for the rest of my life if He would let me live and make my mommy stop crying. This promise to God to be a good little girl started a different pattern in my life. I started trying to be good on my own, not realizing for a long time that only God can make us good.

Staying in bed was so hard for me because I was a very active and busy child. It was difficult for my family, too, since Mom had to care for a new baby brother, Joe, a three-year-old brother, Dan, my older brother, George, and me, too. My dad and brothers were only allowed short weekly visits to my bedroom, so books became my friends. There was no other form of entertainment in Munday in those days – no TV, nothing for kids on the radio. So my mother scoured all the libraries nearby for books that I could read. That's when I came to love reading – and I still do.

One interesting result of my reading was that when I later took an achievement test, I made a perfect score – a college level score – which was quite remarkable for a child of my age. The superintendent called my mom, who had been substitute teaching occasionally, and asked if she had gotten a copy of the test in advance, and coached me. I remember how upset my mother was to be asked such a thing. She was one of the most honorable women that I've ever known, and of course she didn't and wouldn't have coached me even if she had seen that test. That was one of my first real lessons in the meaning of honor and integrity.

There was a lady in our church who offered to give me piano lessons. She was a widow with a really sweet side – and my parents gave her a lot of things, including milk and eggs. So, in return, she asked them if she could teach me piano lessons, and I did learn to play the piano fairly well. But I also wanted to take voice lessons. I didn't sing great, but I liked to sing. And I wanted to perform. I was asked to sing "How Much Is That Doggie in the Window?" Daddy couldn't carry a tune in a bucket. He really sang horribly. It was just awful, croaking, so he didn't think I could sing, either. He was just mortified that I was going to be singing at the Methodist church in front of all these whoopdy-doopty people, and he would have to put on his suit and tie and go with mother and me to the recital. I played my little piano piece. Then, when I got up to sing "How Much Is That Doggie in the Window?" Daddy slumped down in his seat and hid in embarrassment because his daughter was up there trying to sing. I thought I sounded pretty good – kind of cute – but I didn't know that he thought so. I was in third grade when I found that out, maybe eight years old.

The years of my childhood were idyllic and fun, filled with family, church, and school, a mom and dad who loved me, and brothers who tormented me. It was a very normal and special farm existence. I learned to drive sitting on my daddy's lap on his Ford tractor and grew into young womanhood early. My brother and I sold the farm produce like watermelons and cantaloupes, which taught us the value of money and hard labor. My parents gave my older brother and me much responsibility, and we embraced it with fervor.

But I did have an irrational fear of bugs. While many people are afraid of snakes, we had a lot of experience with snakes at our house, and I wasn't afraid of snakes because whenever there was a snake – it didn't matter if it was a chicken snake, a rattlesnake, or a water moccasin – my mom would take the hoe and just go chop its head off.

My fear of bugs came because my dad was bitten all over with ants once – and he just didn't feel them. He had really tough skin so he didn't feel the ant bites very much, and he apparently had so much venom in his body from all the ant bites and wasp stings that he couldn't feel. His body collected the venom until one time he got bites all over him and he had to go to the hospital, and I was afraid that he was going to die.

Another time, as a child, my friend and I were crawling around after Sunday night church. We had an ice cream supper at a friend's house, and my friend got bitten by a black widow spider and died because we couldn't get her to the hospital in time. So even today, if I see an insect, even just a roach, I'm absolutely out of my mind. I can just hardly bear it, even though I know that roaches can't hurt you.

This has led to some amusing experiences and relationships in my adult life. For example, when I became the principal of one school, I had this great custodian who was just precious, and I said "Sepherino, I will take care of the snakes, and you take care of the roaches." And he laughed and said, "Missy, that'll be just great. That's a really good deal for me."

Later, when I had a school that was on a bayou, a snake crawled up under the Big Toy and, of course, I had to take care of it. My assistant principal was a man, but he was afraid of it. But anytime there was a roach, I would scream and the custodian would come running.

I grew up excelling in school, becoming president of my class in grade six. I remember vividly the class officers' photo that appeared in the school annual. I was standing with the three other male officers, towering over them. I was almost full-grown physically in sixth grade, so they came about to my waist. My older brother jumped off the school bus the day the annuals were distributed and ran screaming in the house, informing Mom that girls were not supposed to be presidents. Of course, he was president of his class and their photo did not look dumb. What I didn't realize was that he was slower-developing physically, and I actually was taller and weighed more at age eleven than he, even though he was older than me. Mom very gently reprimanded George and told him that girls could certainly be presidents of organizations. I was to have many future opportunities.

My brothers teased me, calling me "big cow" and "whale blubber" and phrases like that, that brothers make up. That was my biggest torment – and that teasing made me feel inadequate in some ways, and of course with my strong personality I reacted and fought back. I hated my freckles, and they teased me about them. I had thick glasses, too. I thought I was too big and very ugly. My dad thought I was pretty. I looked a lot like Dad, but because he thought I would get a big head about it, he would say, "Missy, you're the prettiest girl I've got!" And then he would slap his leg and laugh. His teasing and my brothers' made me feel that I was ugly and funny looking, feelings that are very hard to get past when you're an adolescent.

CHAPTER 2

Frugality, Fun, and Frito Lay

When I was quite young, oil was found on our property, but our way of life did not change. Except for my dad purchasing more land and hiring more farm workers, no one would have ever known that we were financially better off. My parents were both products of the Great Depression and very frugal. My mom purchased my baby brother's clothes from a Christian family in town where the grandparents, a bachelor uncle and a childless uncle and aunt, all worked in the same grocery business. They pooled their money and bought their son's clothes at Neiman Marcus in Dallas. These hand-me-downs were better than most of what we could have purchased at our one department store in Munday.

When my youngest brother started first grade, he got in a fight because one of the other children called him a "little rich kid." Joe had replied, "We ain't rich. I don't even have a pair of new shoes." The principal called my mom and asked her if she didn't think that she and Lonnie (my dad) had overdone their frugality a bit.

My parents were so afraid that we would think more of ourselves than we ought to think. They definitely believed in "jerking the rug out from under us to keep us humble." My dad would say, at almost every meal, "We may not have enough taters to last out the year." The potatoes grown on my father's farms furnished potatoes for Lay's Potato Chip Factory, so we certainly had enough potatoes to eat. It was just his way of reminding us that we needed to remember the source of all the good things we had, even the produce we raised.

We always discussed items of great importance at meal-times where everyone heard everyone else's business, and indigestion was assured. After Joe was called to the principal's office for getting in that fight, at supper Joe asked my mother, "Mom, if we aren't poor, could I have my very own brand new pair of shoes?" Mom took him the next day to the Fair Store in Munday, and he got his shoes.

A few years later, Joe went with Dad and Mom and me to the orthodontist in Wichita Falls where I went every two weeks to try to correct a prognathic jaw. Joe told Dr. Stanley, "When I grow up I'm going to do nothing, just like my daddy. But I'm going to wear a suit instead of overalls when I ride around in my pickup truck and tell all the farm workers what to do!"

My mom went white at supper when Dad said, "One day you will all thank me for what I'm about to do. I'm going to find work elsewhere for most of our farm hands, and you kids and I are going to work the farm." So from then on, my brothers and I worked before and after school to help make our large farm operation successful. Our parents did not want us to think we were rich and that we did not need to work. In the summer when I was in high school, I ran the vegetable sheds my dad owned where potatoes were culled and sent to market. We all learned to work hard.

Once when Dad and I went to Wichita Falls, I told him I needed a gown for an upcoming special event, so he took me shopping and we bought this beautiful turquoise evening gown. I thought it was the most beautiful dress I'd ever seen. But it was strapless, and my mother was horrified when we got home that my shoulders and a little bit of my bosom were showing, so she made a wrap to go around my shoulders so that I would not be showing off too much of my body when I was being the mistress of ceremonies. With Mom, modesty was a must.

The same was true of Dad. He would not allow me to wear skimpy clothing, not even a swimsuit. As a teenager, I made myself some shorts because I loved to sew, but I was only allowed to wear them in the house, and if someone came to the door, I had to put on my long pants to answer the door. Yet Daddy was reasonable about it, too, because when I played basketball, he let me wear shorts, knowing it would be embarrassing for me to wear long pants when everybody else was wearing shorts.

When we were young, Dad smoked cigarettes. He said that he had learned to smoke cigarettes when he was eight or nine years old, because he would go out with his older cousins who smoked. So sometimes Dad would come home smelling like smoke. And my grandmother accused him of smoking, so he told us, "I figured that if I was accused, I might as well do it." That was an important lesson for me, to be careful what I accused people of doing, because they might use the accusation as an excuse to go ahead and do whatever it was.

By the time Dad was about forty, we were learning that lung cancer might be caused by smoking, so we would cry and beg Daddy to quit smoking. He smoked Lucky Strikes, and only one or two a day, so it wasn't like he chain smoked. But one day he said to my brother, "You all have been wanting me to quit smoking, and I found these cigs in your pocket, son. So I'll make you a deal. If you will quit and not smoke again unless you tell me, I will try to quit. I will also need you to help me teach your little brothers and sister not to smoke." My brother agreed, and Daddy kept his word.

But before that, when we were traveling to Wichita Falls, I had asked him once, "Daddy, just let me have a smoke. I think I'd like to smoke one of those cigarettes." He looked at me, lit up one, and handed it to me. I took a puff. He thought I looked very sophisticated (he thought I had smoked before, which I never had). But he didn't say a word. He just kept driving. When he didn't get upset, I didn't want to or need to smoke anymore. That's the only time I ever puffed a cigarette, because I thought: *Well, if he's not going to get upset, why should I do it?* That was another good lesson, too – when your children do things or threaten to do things, do not overreact, and they may just decide there is a better way.

I continued to excel in school and learned to cook and sew at home in addition to taking home economics in high school. Some of my work was entered in a state contest, and I won a state award. I was a class officer, played in the band and was an officer there. I also was captain of the girls' basketball team. We were pretty good, ending up second in the state in our division in my junior year. I did not realize that all this success came from God and not from my own efforts, for this was the period of time where I was trying to achieve everything and to be good on my own. I graduated from Munday High School in 1961 as valedictorian of my class, giving my valedictory address in the same auditorium where my mom had given her valedictory address in 1930.

In the summertime we had vegetable sheds, and it was my job to get the potatoes out and sold to Lay's Potato Chip Factory. Well, one summer all our helpers were picked up and taken to Mexico or something – anyway there was nobody to help, so I just went and got the football team and the pep squad down there to help me. I fed them coffee, and made sandwiches, and we got those potatoes processed and out in short order.

During my high school years, I was always leading. Once there was a rebellion among the students after a school board member's daughter had gotten a spanking by the coach, which I thought she deserved. Spanking was legal in those days. I thought the kid was spoiled rotten and that she had done wrong. But a bunch of the kids decided that what had happened was not a good thing and they wanted to get rid of this coach, so they were going to picket the school. Their plan was to go downtown and make a scene. Well, when my dad got wind of that, he drove to town and found the superintendent standing there, taking in what was going on. "Is Sara here?" Daddy asked. "Heck, no," the superintendent answered. "She's got too much sense to be here. She'd never be here. She's at the school keeping the rest of them occupied."

Anyway, it seems like from the time I was a little girl I was always telling people what to do, but through the years I learned the difference between bossing people and leading them. As I've studied this quality in others, and thought about my own development, I've concluded that leaders are not just born, they are made, and that – even if they don't realize it – God has a lot to do with the result. I do credit my mom with tempering my exuberance, helping me to be more sensitive, and giving me the basis of discipline. My personality and character come from my dad, but the way I do things – quickly, well, right, and without leaving a big mess behind – these came from my mom.

Mom was the stabilizing force in our home; Daddy was the colorful one. He was a wonderful father, but Mother was an iron hand in a velvet glove. Our character and values – I have three wonderful, successful brothers – those values were lived out by our father but implanted in us by our mother. She loved God. She loved mankind. She was a servant, a true servant.

She didn't let us throw anything away. If I put things in the trash, she would pull them out and either keep them or take them down to Goodwill. She was tiny, maybe ninety-five pounds, but as I write this draft she has just led the parade in my fiftieth high school class reunion as the oldest living graduate of our high school. She led the parade riding in a Model T Ford, behind the grand marshal, who was also in a Model T. She graduated eighty years ago, as valedictorian of her class, which I never even knew until Daddy told me. As I write this, Mom still lives today at ninety-eight years of age in the farm home where I was born. Her influence continues.

Mom was very smart, but she never bragged about that. In fact, she never bragged about anything. She was very reserved and conservative. She didn't talk about herself; she didn't boast about Daddy, or the farm, or even her kids. As I describe her right now, I envision her working on her daily crossword puzzle, and getting every single entry right without consulting a dictionary or any other source of information.

She was Daddy's helpmate. She lived with him almost seventy-three years, and when he died she said she had lost her best friend, that losing him was the hardest thing she had ever experienced. She was the oldest of seven children, and she was more of a mother to the rest than her mother was. Her mother was fifteen when Mom was born, so Mom helped raise her siblings, because that was where her help was needed during that period of her life. I'm so glad that in her later years we could become the best of friends.

My dad was my hero. At his funeral, my brothers and I told funny stories. One of our favorites involved his hearing aid. As he grew older, his hearing was declining, his eyesight was failing, and he couldn't walk very well; in short, the way he would put it would be, "My parts quit working." Toward the end of his life, one day he couldn't find his hearing aid, so Mother made him get in the den and she dressed him down – took his pants off, took his boots off and shook them out, shook out his shirt, undressed him all the way to his shirt and socks – but the hearing aid was nowhere to be found.

"Well," he said, "I'm just going to go right down to the Dairy Queen and have coffee with the group." He and his friends went to the Dairy Queen every day and sat at what they called "the truth table." So Daddy went down there (it was only about a mile and a half from home), and he sat down at the truth table next to the undertaker, Ritchie, whom we had known all his life (and who was standing in the back of the sanctuary during the funeral, listening). Telling this story was one of the ways we thanked Ritchie for all the wonderful things that he had done for our family, not only then, but in the past.

When Daddy sat down at the truth table, Ritchie said, "Lonnie, I can hear your hearing aid."

"No, no, no, you can't," Daddy replied. "Sara [my mom] looked, and she couldn't find it. She took all my clothes off and couldn't find it. You must be hearing something else."

But then the other men chimed in, all of them confirming that they, too, could hear that hearing aid. So they followed Daddy out to the pick-em-up truck to make sure it didn't shake out of his clothes while he hobbled out there. They watched him get in, then called Mom and told her to meet him at the pickup when he got home. They told her to watch him come into the house and that she should look again, because they all could hear its high-pitched sound.

So mother dressed Daddy down again – shirt, pants, cuffs, boots, the whole nine yards – but still couldn't find that hearing aid. Finally, though, when she unsnapped the top snap of his boxer shorts, there it was, nestled in his navel!

Well, for the next few weeks, Daddy would tell this story, and he would slap his leg and laugh – I can hear it now in my mind. "Sissy," he would chuckle, "did you hear what happened to my hearing aid? Mom found it in my belly button. Ha. Ha. Can you imagine that? How it got in there I'll never know! Ha. Ha." And then he would slap his leg again for good measure. I never counted how many times he told me that story, because it didn't matter that he was repeating himself. Every time he told it, we all laughed again. He taught us all to laugh at ourselves.

Another time, after I had married Frank (which I'll talk about in the last part of the book), Frank and I had driven to Munday to try to discern if the assisted living home there would be a good place for his mother, who had Alzheimer's for the last thirteen years of her life. We were considering Munday because we knew the facility and the people, and we loved them and the way they took care of their residents – it's a special place.

Frank and I were talking to Mom and Dad about it, and Daddy said, "Let's just run up there and see what you think." Now this was around 1985, when Daddy was still healthy himself. But he insisted on going with us, saying that he would just sit in the car and wait while we checked things out.

While he was sitting in the car outside that facility, my two twin nieces came running past. They were sophomores or juniors at the time, and key members of a track team that won Class A division in Texas several years in a row. So there they were in their jogging suits, working out, when they saw Daddy sitting in Frank's car. "Bop, Bop" (that's what they called him), "What are you doing sitting out here in this car?"

And he replied, "It's just such a shame. Sissy's about to throw me in the nursing home!"

"But Bop, Bop," they said. "Aunt Sara wouldn't do that. She especially wouldn't do that without talking to her brothers!"

"Well, she did this time," he insisted, with a straight face. "And that's why she's in there, just trying to put me away."

Just about then, Frank and I emerged from the facility, having decided that it wouldn't be so good to move Mother Eggleston that far from her home. And I saw him talking with the girls, so, surmising that he was pulling some kind of prank, I said, "Daddy, what are you doing?"

When Angie and April told me what he had said, I said, "Daddy, you big miff. We were in there talking about Frank's mother!"

And he slapped his leg and laughed, just like always, and then he said, "If only I could have squeezed out just one tear – just a little one – I would have had them convinced. And they would have felt sorry for me! Ha. Ha."

One other story that fits in here has to do with Frank, and one of his earlier experiences with Daddy. When Frank first came to meet my family, before we were married, Daddy took him around to see the various farms and ranches. As they were driving through Munday, they came to a stop sign. Daddy just drove right through it, without slowing down, since nobody was coming from the other direction. Well, Frank put his feet down like he was bracing himself or driving from the right side of the pickup. When Daddy saw that, he said, "Son, you just have to know something. In Munday, Texas, the stop signs are for visitors!"

So he was always having fun, always lighting up the room – even at his own funeral. And we were all absolutely sure that he would have approved!

Sara Eggleston

Part II

Living In Fear

Sara Eggleston

CHAPTER 3

Blind Love, Bounced Checks, and Bad Company

I met my first husband when I was sixteen, at church when he came to Munday from Abilene to visit. His grandmother had passed away, and I took a German chocolate cake to their house for guests to eat who attended the funeral. I fell head over heels in love, and my life was never the same again. He was from a good family who knew my parents. He should have been exactly what I needed.

What I did not see until it was much too late was that he had a character flaw that would ruin my life and eventually ruin our marriage and his own life. My dad had taught me to "read" people the way you read books. He said to me, "Sissy, if you do not learn to read people, you are going to be in trouble about ninety percent of the time." My future husband kept who he was and what he was cov-

41

ered up, and I was so in love that I did not see it. I thought I was ugly, and I was just so glad that somebody thought I was special.

We married after my first semester at Abilene Christian College. He had joined the Army, so we drove to our new home in El Paso, Texas, where he was stationed at Fort Bliss. I wept when I saw this barren place, but I also cried when I moved away a year later. I began learning that we must bloom where we are planted and that beauty comes in all different forms – that even the desert has its own kind of beauty.

When we arrived at our little apartment close to the base, I found evidence of another woman's things in the house. My husband claimed that this woman had lived there alone before we married. I later found out that she had lived there with my husband even after we were engaged to be married.

I was surprised when my husband bought a second-hand car and a television that we could not afford. After all, we already had a car that was paid for and we could not afford payments on a television or a car. Very often, we did not have enough money to buy groceries at the commissary toward the end of the month, and there was no food in the house. In spite of that fact, he once invited a buddy for lunch without telling me. We were having chicken and dumplings made with two chicken wings that I had saved when I had fried chicken earlier in the week. But he was the husband, and I was his wife, so I didn't make a fuss about it.

I occupied myself with housework such as making curtains from scratch, still believing that everything would be all right. I enrolled in Texas Western to continue my education. I caught the bus by our house and rode it to school. We placed membership at a church in El Paso, and one of the elders came to me one Sunday and told me that my husband had stolen money out of the collection plate. Of course, I did not believe him. After all, I figured, who would do such a thing. There had to be some mistake. The blinders of my love for him kept me from seeing the evidences of weak and corrupted character in the man that I had married.

After a few months, my husband was sent to Fort Dix, New Jersey, so I returned to Abilene, Texas, to continue my studies at Abilene Christian. I lived with his parents during that time. His mother was good to me and a wonderful person in general. She taught me about the Holy Spirit and His role in living the Christian life. At night, the three of us – my mother-in-law, father-in-law, and I – would play bridge, to which they had introduced me.

I'll never forget how one night during that period my husband called me from New Jersey. "I got drunk," he said through his crocodile tears, which I thought were genuine. "I got drunk and I committed adultery. I'm so sorry. You should just go get a divorce."

Of course I was absolutely heartbroken, but since I had never even tasted alcohol and certainly did not know the effects of inebriation, I told him that I was sure that he would never have done this if he had not been drunk. I pretended this never happened and put it out of my mind. Not long thereafter, he was assigned to Greenland. But after only a few months in Greenland, he was reassigned to New Jersey due to an injury that, in hindsight, I'm confident he faked. He could fake just about anything.

I did not join him in New Jersey because I knew that I needed to finish my college studies. This was one of the few times during all the years we were married where my God-given and mother-instilled intuition and father-instilled perception preserved me and kept me on a path that would leave me with some options in the case of disaster. For, had I moved to New Jersey to be with him, I seriously doubt that I would have emerged from the chaos ahead with a college degree and some way to take care of myself. By the time my husband had finished his three-year tour of duty with Uncle Sam, I had completed my teaching degree and had gotten a job at Jackson Elementary School teaching fifth grade.

My husband's continuing irresponsibility with money and his irregular patterns of living were getting worse, and my eyes were beginning to open. When I found *Playboy* magazines under the seat of his car, he claimed that a friend had left them there. Once when I was shopping at Gibson's Discount Store (like a small Sam's), I tried to pay for the purchase with a check. The store manager came over and told me, right there at the checkout stand and loud enough for others to hear, that we had bounced several checks, so they could no longer allow me to pay for purchases by check. As it happened, my Bible professor was behind me in line. I was so embarrassed and simply did not understand how such a thing could be true, since I had learned from childhood to manage the checkbook well. I left the groceries on the counter and headed home. We had a joint bank account, and my checkbook showed we had money. I had not known about the bounced checks, though I'm not sure how my husband kept the facts from me for so long. When I got home, the water had been turned off because of another bad check. I was horrified and ashamed.

I had been raised in a home where we trusted each other and told the truth. The horror, shame, and embarrassment that I felt in my new situation were so big for me because my father's word was his bond. When he told you he would do something, you didn't need a contract to sign. That's the way I was raised, and that's the way I am now.

Back then, I thought that the worst things that could possibly happen to a marriage were that your husband would commit adultery, that he would find someone else, or that he would commit a crime and have to go to jail. I couldn't imagine surviving the shame and disgrace of such things happening, and so in those years I constantly lived with shame and disgrace, and in fear, asking God to show me, every minute, what to do.

Sometimes the pain from living like that was so strong, and my focus on "survival" was so intense that my brain didn't seem to work. It wasn't the same kind of pain that might have come from a disease or my fear that I was going to lose my sight, which seemed likely at the time due to a condition that I had. In terms of that kind of pain, I knew in my heart of hearts that God would see me through – that if I lost my sight, I could make it with His help, since many people have made it without their sight. I didn't want to have to do that, but I believed that if that was what He allowed, He would help me live with it.

But the kind of life my husband's actions immersed me in was so shameful and so antithetic to the life I'd known on the farm that I just felt dirty. Instead of life being stable, truthful, and trustworthy, it seemed that everything had become unstable, untruthful, and untrustworthy. And some days I was so frightened and burdened that I would have to make my legs walk. Strange as it sounds now, I actually had to pick them up with my hands and put them one foot in front of the other to make them work, because the pain inside of me was so strong. I didn't recognize, of course, the extreme seriousness of this symptom, since a reaction like that to psychic pain is certainly a symptom that one is headed for one level of insanity or another.

Then, in the midst of all that chaos, I got pregnant. In those days in Texas, you could not start a new semester as a teacher if you knew you were pregnant – that was the law. I was terrified that my principal would find out, because my income from teaching was the only thing that was sustaining our life, financially, and my mind, psychologically. And so at mid-term of that year I had to resign, and Camille was born the following May.

Well, my principal did not want to lose me, so he hired a friend of mine, whose husband was going to Cornell, to take my classroom. My principal liked me and knew I could handle those difficult children. I told him that my husband was in school, and I really had to work. So we left all my things in the room, and my friend replaced me with the understanding that I would try to get my job back later.

When Camille was born, we had been married for five

years. Her lungs collapsed the night she was born due to asthma, and for awhile it was touch and go regarding whether she would ever make it out of the hospital the first time.

When she did, I was afraid that my baby was going to die, and I carried that fear by myself day in and day out. I stayed up every night; we hooked up a device to the bed where I could hear her, and I kept it hooked to my body. But I was afraid to go to sleep in case she might stop breathing in the night. So I stayed up and sewed and made our clothes. I did housework and cooked and cleaned, until about 1 AM most nights, only sleeping maybe two to three hours a night for a long, long time.

Simply put, I was terrified that she was going to die because she was always, always sick. She had thirty-seven trips to the hospital before she was five. Her fragile hold on life was a bigger terror for me than my own life being in danger, because I loved her so much and felt so helpless. And I knew we couldn't pay. I was so afraid that a check would bounce without my knowing, we would get to the hospital with another emergency, and they wouldn't let us in. That was a constant, nearly immobilizing fear.

Some people die from asthma, but most people don't. I learned later to be thankful that she didn't have leukemia or she wasn't a quadriplegic or have some disease that couldn't be overcome. And, of course, I learned later that diet makes such a difference in connection with any disease, but I didn't know that then, and very few medical professionals did, either.

With my degree of anxiety over Camille (in addition to the other things), I learned how so many people may end up in mental institutions because they worry about what might happen instead of focusing on what really is happening, and learning to live in the present. Someone stuck in anxiety might not be able to find their keys in the morning, for example. While most people would be able to focus on finding those keys, a person in this state of mind might think, "Oh, my goodness. I'm going to be late for work, and then I'm going to get fired. And after I get fired, I'm going to be unemployed and unable to pay the mortgage, so I'll lose my house, and my car, and everything I have or care about. I'll end up on the street, living in a shipping crate, or maybe in a homeless shelter and begging for money on a street corner just to make it!"

Thinking like this can become a pattern triggered by just about anything. My main trigger was Camille's health. I worried about it *all* the time. I was just terrified – even when she was well. I could not enjoy her being well because I was afraid she was going to get sick, and, of course, within a day or two she did get sick again. If it wasn't daily, it was weekly – at least as long as I attended church, which had always been one of my main sources of support and strength.

She was such a beautiful baby and so good. She was the most precious thing in my life. But it seemed that everyone takes themselves and their children to church sick, so when I would take Camille to worship, she would catch something and become very ill within twenty-four hours. So, reluctantly, I stopped taking her to church and had worship via TV with Dr. Robert Schuller and his "Hour of Power" each Sunday.

As Camille's health deteriorated, she spent a great deal of time in the hospital or under the oxygen tent at our home. Her wonderful doctor, Dr. Stanton Barron, would come to our home to see her and never send me a bill. He would rock her in the middle of the night and give her a shot to clear her lungs. He knew I could not pay. I will always remember and treasure his kindness. But his visits were like islands of calm and protection in my personal gathering storm. Dr. Barron suggested that I take Camille off dairy products and put her on soy milk, considering the possibility that dairy products can exacerbate allergies and asthma. I refused. I was a farm girl who had grown up going to the barn with her daddy and milking the cows. The idea of drinking soy milk instead of cow's milk was as foreign to me as the thought of moving to China. I would later learn that this change might have made a huge difference. But at that point I was still living in a black and white world that was filled with fear.

I was frantic and did not know where to turn. My life was in shambles with an irresponsible, unfaithful husband and a sick baby. I felt the weight of the world on my shoulders. I was not depending on God, and I was about to go crazy. I had been a good little girl since my own illness so many years earlier, and I had tried to be a good wife and mother, but nothing was working. I could not figure out what to do or what had gone wrong. I did not yet know that it is not what happens to you but how you take it and what you make of it that makes the difference. I did not understand that bad things happen to good people, yet God is still in charge and overseeing it all. It's not a matter of our control, but His, and it's not a matter of how good we can be on our own, but of how good we are because He is our good Father as a result of our faith in Christ. In the back of my mind, I knew the truth of Ephesians 2:20, "He is able to do all that we ask or think," yet my focus continued to be on what I could do to regain control and change things for the better.

I thought we had to have my teaching salary to pay our bills, so I had a nanny come to our home to care for Camille once I was able to get my old teaching job back. This lovely lady gave Camille a certain tenderness, stability, and a calm spirit, which wonderfully offset my daily struggle against the chaos that was threatening to undo me.

It wasn't easy to regain my job. When it came time to return, the old bachelor personnel director of that school said to me, "You don't really want to come back to work, do you? I don't think I can hire you back, and I'm not required to do so."

"But I *have* to work," I replied. "And I want to work at Jackson Elementary. Not only so, Mr. Fitzgerald wants me back. Sure, I could take the job that I've been offered in Wiley, teaching English and coaching seventh grade girls' basketball, but I wouldn't be near as good at that as I would be here, teaching fourth grade, and helping out with all those problem students."

"I'm sure you don't want to leave your baby," he said. It was no secret how sick Camille had been.

"No, sir. I don't want to leave my baby," I replied. "And I don't want to work outside the home, but I *have* to work so we can eat. Didn't you ever do anything that you needed to do instead of what you wanted to do? I have to have a job. So if you're not going to rehire me today, I'm going to tell the superintendent in Wiley that I will take that position."

After my principal, Mr. Fitzgerald, heard what had happened, he got really mad and stormed over there and forced them to give me my job back. I didn't like having to do it that way, since alienating anybody in upper management wherever you work is never a good idea, but I was in survival mode, and I did whatever it took to keep things going.

What I didn't see was that I was also in grief mode during those years, with all the anger and denial and negotiation and depression that are the stages of grief that have been studied and written about so much since then. For such a long time I was angry but not willing to see what my husband was really like – whether from pride or fear or wishing or hoping that he would change, I don't know. That was the denial part. Then I tried to negotiate with God: "If I'm good, You will reward me by changing him, won't You?" When that didn't work, I became seriously depressed almost to the point of despair. Acceptance, the final stage, was still many years, and a lot more grief, away. Without doubt, during that particular time I was not practicing what Alcoholics Anonymous members pray at every meeting, an adaptation of the prayer originally penned by Reinhold Niebuhr: "God, grant me the serenity to accept the things I cannot change; courage to change the things I can; and wisdom to know the difference."

Instead, each time something bad happened, I would

think: *Oh, I can't believe it. I can't handle this. I can't stand it.* Truthfully, the pain was too strong for my brain. In fact, the residual pain, as I have relived this in order to write about it, is still so strong that when I tried to put it on paper for the first time, I had to vomit.

I felt fragmented and frantic all the time. Our finances got worse, and my husband ran away from the problems. I was called from California and told that he had tried to commit suicide. They had pumped his stomach and had him in a hospital. My father-in-law went to get him, as I could not leave our baby and my job. He was placed in a psychiatric hospital for treatment, but the doctors could find nothing wrong with him. His IQ was so high, he was able to fake emotions and give answers that were correct. When our problems got straightened out, he seemed to be okay for awhile. But then the next catastrophe happened.

I will never forget how, when Camille was in the oxygen tent at our home with another severe asthma attack, the police came to the door. The officer told me that our Chevrolet Impala had been abandoned on the edge of Abilene and there was blood all over the inside of the door. My husband had disappeared.

I was absolutely terrified! Reporters, who had heard the story on their scanners, had followed the police to my door and wanted to know the details – when I didn't even know the details myself. My husband was from a prominent Abilene family and anything they did was newsworthy – at least the media vultures thought so. I called my precious mother-in-law and she came over to watch Camille, and I went on to school to teach my thirty-two fourth-grade students. I had to keep my job now more than ever, I reasoned. Besides, staying occupied with that kept me as sane as I could be.

My husband had left me behind to clear up his debts, sell our home, and take care of our child. No one knew where he was. I had a deep feeling that he was alive and just avoiding his responsibilities. A letter from one of his lovers had been left in the glove compartment of the abandoned car. He told me that I was free and should get a divorce. I did get a legal separation, which was allowed in Texas at the time, but, of course, that didn't really solve anything. He was missing for over a year.

My dad kept a tiny old trailer close to the Abilene Christian University campus for students that he funded to use for living quarters. This trailer was empty. Camille and I moved in after the house sold, and we put our furniture in storage. Though the trailer was a godsend, during this period I lost touch with the God who had sent it. I felt He had abandoned me. I had a sick child, a husband who had disappeared, and no money. I was absolutely terrified that I would take Camille to the hospital and they would refuse to treat her because I had not paid my bill, so I tried to pay our medical bills before I purchased food.

In the midst of that darkness, as I began trying to make some sense out of the mess of my life, I found two books that I still use as references today: *How to Win Over Worry*, by Dr. John Edmund Haggai and *Beyond Our Selves*, by Catherine Marshall. These books helped me get back into the Word of God and begin praying, asking God why He had forgotten about me. As an answer, God sent me one of the greatest gifts of my life. One night after putting Camille in bed, I sat in that little trailer house, asking God to show me that He loved me. In my mind, I "heard" these words: "Go call 'Laura.'"

Laura was a former college friend whom I had seen at church the previous Sunday with her handsome husband and three precious children. I remember thinking how lovely it was that she had such a stable family and such a nice spouse to help her. I argued with the "voice" in my head, saying, "It's past 10 PM already – too late to call." My mom taught me to never call after 9 PM.

But the voice would not stop. When it got past 11 PM, I rationalized: "I cannot call Laura this late, for sure. Besides, I do not have her phone number." And suddenly I remembered the Old Testament story of Samuel and how God spoke to him in his sleep. So I gathered my courage and called my sister-in-law, Becky, who stayed up every night past midnight. I knew she would have Laura's phone number from Ladies' Bible Class. I asked Becky for Laura's number, without telling her why I was asking, especially at that hour. I wrote the number down and went to bed.

Then the voice became a tremendous pounding in my mind, to the point where I simply had to call. So I called, with my apology all ready to give. But when I started to apologize for calling at midnight, Laura burst into tears and sobbed into the phone, telling me that her husband had left her and her three children, and that since 10 PM she had been clutching a butcher knife, ready to slit her wrists and kill herself. She said, "I have been praying since then that someone would help me and give me a reason to live."

There was no denying that God had answered my prayer and showed me that He loved me more than I could ever imagine by trusting me with another person's life. Yet I almost hadn't listened. As the days ahead got worse, I often looked back on the night when I had heard the voice of God, and that memory reassured me that He would see me through. Even though my faith wavered and needed to be bolstered in the years ahead, I never again doubted that our God is real, and that He is able to deliver those who are His own.

Sara Eggleston

CHAPTER 4

A Reign of Terror

C atherine Marshall's chapter on forgiveness in *Beyond Our Selves* was absolutely phenomenal for me because there was this woman in the book, whose husband had committed adultery, and was still living in the same town as his wife. After a year or two of living this way, he said he was sorry and asked to reconcile, but she said that she could not forgive him. She went to her clergyman, who asked, "Do you want to forgive him?"

"Yes," she replied. "I do, but I cannot."

That was when the priest sketched out a little diagram, in the form of a triangle, with one phrase on each side, something like this:

"I will...."
"To will...."
"The will of God...."

"Many times we wait to act, or even refuse to act, because we aren't feeling the emotional energy we think we need in order to attempt something that is really difficult. But if we give our wills to God," he explained, "then He will supply the emotions that go with the actions. And He will also supply the courage and strength to follow through, for the Scriptures teach that He is working in His children both to will and to work for His good pleasure."

So the woman did, indeed, forgive her wayward husband. They reunited and were able to have a successful marriage.

Well, I thought that I was in a very similar place because my husband wanted to reunite after having been missing for a year. He had committed adultery many times over, and was always "sorry" – but then he would go out and do the same thing again. So I just didn't feel that I could trust him. But after reading this story, I realized that God would supply the emotions if I acted according to His will. So, like the Old Testament character Gideon, I asked God for a sign. Actually, I asked for more than one: that we would have a real house to live in, since the little trailer house was not a suitable place for reuniting a marriage when there is a young daughter living there, too; that he would get a job; and that he would re-enroll in Abilene Christian and finish his studies. When these things happened, we did reunite.

After that, we moved to Dallas. I expected that now the best was yet to come. Little did I know that, comparing my life to that famous short story by Frank Stockton, behind that closed door was not a lady but a terrifying tiger. The reign of terror began when my husband became a witness to an interstate crime that involved the Mafia. Fraudulent school bonds had been used as collateral for an apartment purchase that his company was making. Our daughter, Camille, and I were put in a witness protection program, our beautiful Dallas home was confiscated for unpaid back taxes, and we were on the run, being moved from place to place for our own protection.

That year, 1975, was filled with events more horrible than any simple farm girl could possibly imagine. I was called by the FBI soon after the protection program started. "Your husband has been beaten," they said, "and is in a hospital in Oklahoma." I was flown to see him – and seeing him beaten beyond recognition filled my heart and life with even more fear. His face was like mush. He had gotten a hernia from having been kicked, and he had to have surgery. I could only imagine what might happen if the same people who had done this might find Camille and me.

A few weeks later my mother-in-law was murdered and my father-in-law was shot twice. I had come to love Martha so much. She was such a wonderful and charming woman, a music teacher with a beautiful voice. I attended her funeral with an FBI agent by my side. I was devastated, since she had been one of my best friends through the early years of my marriage to her son. Knowing her son better than I knew him, she seemed to understand my concerns and was willing to listen and love me without defending him.

My father-in-law was accused and later convicted of the murder, and sent to prison for life. The jury believed that he had lost his mind because he'd lost all his money by investing it with his son. To this day, I don't know if he did it, or if the Mafia killed Martha, though the timing of it all was really suspicious. Sometimes I wanted to die, myself. And I wanted my husband dead. Not that I would kill him, of course. I just wanted him not to be able to use and manipulate and hurt any more people, and I wondered, *Why does he keep living – when his wonderful mother is dead?* It was all very, very confusing.

I had to fall back on what I'd been taught – the only thing that was absolutely trustworthy was the Lord and His Word. My mother had taught me Scriptures while I sat on the linoleum floor of the kitchen and she churned the butter or made the bread. She would teach me verses, and the names of the books of the Bible, and we would say them in order. Sometimes my brother and I would be playing there on the floor, before we were old enough to go to school, and we would take turns reciting the stories of Adam and Eve, and Cain and Abel, Seth, Noah's Ark, Abraham, Isaac, Jacob and Joseph, Gideon, Samson, Ruth, Joshua and Moses, Jonah, Daniel and his friends Shadrach, Meshach and Abednego, Elijah, David and his friend, Jonathan, and so forth. Then we would go on to the New Testament and the stories of John the Baptist, Jesus and the disciples, Stephen, the apostle Paul, his friend Barnabas, and his doctor, Luke . . . Peter, James, and John and so forth through the Bible, alternating who told which story as we went, and sometimes acting them out rather dramatically for preschoolers.

Often in the dark, at night, I recited Psalm 23 (from the King James Version, which was the version of my youth, and is easier to memorize due to the cadence of the language of that day):

> "The LORD is my shepherd," I would whisper, "I
> shall not want. He maketh me to lie down in green
> pastures: he leadeth me beside the still waters. He
> restoreth my soul: he leadeth me in the paths of
> righteousness for his name's sake. Yea, though I
> walk through the valley of the shadow of death, I
> will fear no evil: for thou art with me; thy rod and
> thy staff they comfort me. Thou preparest a table
> before me in the presence of mine enemies: thou
> anointest my head with oil; my cup runneth over.
> Surely goodness and mercy shall follow me all the
> days of my life: and I will dwell in the house of the
> LORD for ever."

Often I would quote Philippians 4:4-8, which was especially relevant in those moments when I feared I was losing my mind:

> "Rejoice in the Lord always," the apostle Paul had
> written from prison. ". . . again I will say, rejoice!
> Let your gentle *spirit* be known to all men. The Lord
> is near. Be anxious for nothing, but in everything by
> prayer and supplication with thanksgiving let your
> requests be made known to God. And the peace of
> God, which surpasses all comprehension, will guard
> your hearts and your minds in Christ Jesus. Finally,
> brethren, whatever is true, whatever is honorable,
> whatever is right, whatever is pure, whatever is

lovely, whatever is of good repute, if there is any excellence and if anything worthy of praise, dwell on these things" (NASB).

I clung to the truth of verses like, "I can do all things through Christ which strengtheneth me," and passages like Paul's prayer in Ephesians 3:

"That he would grant you, according to the riches of his glory, to be strengthened with might by his Spirit in the inner man; that Christ may dwell in your hearts by faith; that ye, being rooted and grounded in love, may be able to comprehend with all saints what is the breadth, and length, and depth, and height; and to know the love of Christ, which passeth knowledge, that ye might be filled with all the fulness of God. Now unto him that is able to do exceeding abundantly above all that we ask or think, according to the power that worketh in us, unto him be glory in the church by Christ Jesus throughout all ages, world without end. Amen."

I found courage, not only in the biblical examples of the life of faith, but in knowing that, "For God hath not given us the spirit of fear; but of power, and of love, and of a sound mind."

Through it all, I found hope in knowing that, even when things seemed to be about to crash and burn, He was bearing me up on eagles' wings, and that the promise of Isaiah 40:30-31 applied specifically to me: "Even the youths shall faint and be weary, and the young men shall utterly fall: But they that wait upon the LORD shall renew their strength; they shall mount up with wings as eagles; they shall run, and not be weary; and they shall walk, and not faint."

My mother and I had an interesting conversation at about this time. I asked her, "Mom, do you learn as much from thirty to forty as you do from twenty to thirty?"

She replied, "Well, you know, that's really up to you. You've always been pretty smart, Sissy. But you're just starting to have good sense."

Finally, my husband gave his testimony in court, and the pressure lifted. Apparently, a hit is lifted when the person is no longer in danger of giving damaging information to those who perpetrated the crime. We settled in Abilene, and I enrolled in a graduate education program to stay sane. When I was studying, I seemed more able to keep my thoughts focused, and I did not think about all that was wrong in my life.

I sold real estate during my graduate study period, and found it interesting that I could make more money doing that a couple mornings a week than I might normally make teaching a year of elementary school. I did well because I knew the people and they knew and trusted me, and many would specifically request my assistance when they called the agency I worked with. They knew that I had not been involved in anything wrong or illegal but that I was a victim. So I was able to supplement our income significantly when I was in graduate school.

Meanwhile, my husband became involved in construction and tried to do high rolling deals once more. The high rolling deals did not work. He, however, still tried to live the life of a man who had money. He was having numerous affairs and even was reported in the newspaper as having witnessed a robbery while he was in a hotel with his "secretary."

At the end of my graduate school program, we left Abilene, and moved to Houston, where my husband tried again to become involved in things that were on the edge, and none of them worked. I interviewed for teaching positions at several different places. I was offered a job in one district, where a principal who interviewed me asked me how hard I could hit.

"Do you mean, 'Can I spank children?'" Spanking was legal then in Texas. When he nodded, I said, "I taught ten years in Abilene and only had to spank one child – his name was Michael. Of course I called his mother to come up there and be with me when I did it. I gave him two licks – just enough to get his attention. But," I added, "I only did it because I was out of soap. Fortunately, in his case, it did seem to work."

The principal replied, "These children here are really tough. You're going to have to spank them. And when you do, you'll have to hit them really hard to be sure they get it."

Having to beat kids into submission did not appeal to me, so I accepted another job in the Katy school district, where the kids who were assigned to me were really rough. I got them ALL. During the upheaval of the past five years, I had given away all of my classroom stuff, which is the

teacher's next best friend, so I prayed for the Lord to pro-
vide me with materials so I could do my bulletin boards,
so I wouldn't have to spend all my time on them when I
should be working on lessons. As it happened (as God
made it happen), a mom of one of the students from this
very eclectic group of children was a Hallmark representative. She gave me more beautiful bulletin board materials
than I could possibly use. They were prepackaged for every
season, about everything imaginable, and they addressed
every subject that I might cover. I chose materials for each
time during the year, put them in my cabinets, and then
put the box outside my door with a sign for the other
teachers to help themselves. This made me instant friends
with the staff because they got goodies from me – they did-
n't care that the goodies were really from that mother. It
was wonderful.

Very shortly after that year started, there was a lice epi-
demic in the school – and that in my classroom, of course,
with the children from across the tracks, and we were going
to have to take care of this. The teachers were taught how
to part the hair with little sticks and find the lice. And, sure
enough, there were three children with lice – and one very
precious little girl was one of them. She raised her hand in
class, and said, "This isn't a problem about being dirty. I
am a girl scout, and we were out in the woods. I remember
falling off my pallet and out of the sleeping bag, and I was
sure that I got wood ticks and lice in my hair. We are very
clean in our house. It's not about being dirty, but about getting lice in the woods."

Hearing that just broke my heart, but I was still terrified

of the lice – remember my fear of bugs! – so I went home that night and washed and washed and washed my hair, afraid that I had gotten lice, and then I bleached my hair blonde. I thought that bleach would kill anything that had gotten on me, which of course it wouldn't have.

Well, as it happened, the grandchildren of a famous muckraker attended a school near mine, and he got wind of the fact that the Katy schools were infected with lice. So he told us he was coming to our school to interview us. Now my principal knew that I had administrative certification, and that I could handle this fellow. The principal was afraid to be on TV, so he told the TV station that I would be the one to speak for the school in the interview. And here's what I said, "Sir, I know that your grandchildren go to that other school, and I'm sure that they're not dirty. If they got lice you would know that it couldn't possibly be because they were dirty.

"As it happens, one of our infected children got lice, and wood ticks, during a camping trip with the Girl Scouts. So one should be careful, I would think, of stating or even insinuating that the very small number of kids in our district who have been affected by this are just dirty little things whose families don't care or know how to take care of them."

The net result was that instead of doing an exposé on the school district and some of its residents who lived on "the other side of the tracks," the fellow did a nice story about how unfortunate it can be to get lice, and how to diagnose and treat it if it does happen.

Some of the boys in my classroom were just a mess.

Some were as big as me, but they didn't know how to read. So I invited them to stay after school, and taught them how to read. And those kids just fell in love with me and I with them. They would call me at night, and invite me to their parties, and things like that. I had to get their moms to stop them doing that, since it was not appropriate, though I knew it was because they really liked and appreciated me.

One day one of the boys came to school with a new T-shirt upon which was imprinted the image of a gorgeous woman, naked, with her legs wrapped around a chili pot. I said to the boy, "That is really a beautiful woman, but it's not appropriate to wear such clothing in our classroom. Did your daddy buy that for you this weekend at the chili cook-off?"

"Yes, ma'am," he replied.

"Well," I said, "Why don't you step outside the door and turn your shirt inside out, and then we're going to go to the office. We're going to call your daddy and ask him to bring you another shirt."

In this case, I knew his daddy, and I'd been teaching his son how to read, though the daddy had not been very co-operative. So I called the fellow at work and said, "Sir, this is Sara, and I don't know if you know or not, but your son wore that shirt to school today, the one with that beautiful woman on it, with her legs wrapped around a chili pot – you know, the one you bought for him at the chili cook-off last weekend."

On the other end of the phone I heard a gulp, so I added, "She really is a beautiful woman, but it isn't appropriate for him to be wearing that in a sixth-grade school classroom where the boys' hormones are already going crazy. I would really appreciate it if you would bring another shirt for him to wear. We have shirts out there in the bin that he could wear, but I think the lesson would be better for him if you would go home and get him another shirt and bring it to him yourself. Would you do that for me – and for him?"

He took a really big breath and said, "All right." He brought another shirt, and it was amazing the change in that little boy after that . . . and in the dad, too. The cooperation that I had from them from then on was just amazing.

Another time, I looked up and the boys who had been giving me trouble were missing. They had vanished without a sound or a trace. When they didn't return soon, as they might have done had they gone to the restroom, I checked the restroom and the library, and I couldn't find them. Now I was worried, because bad things can happen pretty fast in such a situation. "They have to be playing basketball somewhere," I reassured myself, and thankfully my hunch was right, because in a very short time, all five of them showed up, dripping wet and sweaty.

I asked where they had been. "The restroom," was the first answer.

"No, you weren't. I went down there to look," I replied. "The library."

I said, "No, you weren't. I went down there, too. You've been outside, playing basketball. I can tell; you're dripping wet. I'll tell you what. I think that this is a really good time for you all to just keep playing. There's a playground right beside the school. I'm going to let you go out there and I want you to play for another hour, the whole time, right outside the window where I can watch you. And you cannot stop until I come and get you." I realized this was a rather unconventional solution, but after they *had* to play for another hour, they were ready to study and learn.

Just after the end of that school year, the boys that I had helped rode their bicycles many miles to the school, to bring me a present. I was home when the principal called to tell me the boys had shown up at the school. Since I didn't want them to know where I lived (it was quite close to the school), I walked over to meet them. I surmised that they had stolen it; it was such a beautiful, expensive gift, but for me it was a beautiful experience, and one of my first that happened there that was really, really great.

As my teaching career was progressing, my husband's health was regressing. He was becoming more of a mess emotionally, spiritually, mentally, and physically. I did not know that he was an alcoholic and was drinking vodka every day, all day long. As I look back, I wonder how a person can hide so much of who they are and what they do even when they are in the same household. But he managed. Perhaps it was the denial factor, again – that my heart really didn't want to know what my eyes couldn't miss.

As a result of all the alcohol, the stress of his mom's death, the murder trial and conviction of his father, his twin sister's death from cancer, closing his business, and his high-rolling lifestyle, my husband developed hemorrhagic pancreatitis. His pancreas erupted and "ate" his left lung. In surgery, he was split from his groin to his chest bone twice. He stayed in the hospital intensive care unit for most of that year. By the time this happened, I was an assistant principal in the Katy School District. I got up at 4 AM and drove to the Texas Medical Center before school to check on my husband, leaving our ninth-grade daughter asleep. I would park my car at the medical center so that I could walk through the cancer ward at Texas Children's Hospital before going to Methodist Hospital where he was in ICU. Seeing the courage of these precious children with shaved heads and tiny oxygen equipment attached to their bodies gave me the courage to go on, to believe if they could handle it, I could, too.

I would return home before 6 AM to get our daughter and myself off to school. When my husband was released, he had a heart attack soon afterward and had heart surgery with four bypasses. Once again, the terror of unpaid bills, his unemployability, and the pressures of daily living were more than I could handle. I got a second job at Joske's on the weekends selling women's shoes to help pay rent and to buy our essentials. There I could do a servant's job and sell something that I thought was pretty to other women. It also provided a second income stream to supplement my assistant principal's job.

As life got worse, not better, one Sunday afternoon I cast myself down on the floor of our den in Houston in deepest prayer and despair. In the midst of this, I called my dad and I told him that I did not think I could keep going. He said, "You know, Sissy, I've been worrying about that. Just this morning at the truth table at the Dairy Queen, the guys said, 'That poor girl . . . she's going to go crazy. She can't take much more.'"

I hung up the phone, embarrassed and frustrated that my mental health was the current subject of the truth table. Then I got on my knees and said, "God, I will make it. You've shown me I could make it this far. I will make it; with Your help, I'll make it."

As a result of that prayer, I began to feel the strength and power of God entering my body in a fuller way. I picked up that phone again and called my dad back with this message, "Daddy, you tell those guys in the morning at the Dairy Queen, the ones who diapered me and loved me, that with God's help, I am NOT going to go crazy. I AM going to make it, and we will be all right! Tell them to talk about somebody else!"

A few months later, we had to move again because our leased house had become too expensive for us to afford. Just after we got settled in our next digs, a police officer came to the door with a notice that he had apprehended my husband and taken him to the city jail in downtown Houston. Neighbors told me that my husband had been handcuffed and walked to a police car that had been parked in front of our home. I had just been named to a principal's position and knew that this news would hit the paper of our small and close-knit community with furor. Katy was still a country community at this time. I immediately called our superintendent and told him what had happened. He told me not to worry, this police report would NOT be made public. I don't know how he did it, but the news never hit the paper.

I put on my best clothes, my jewelry, and my fur coat

(it was one of the rare times it was cold in Houston) to drive downtown to the jail. I asked to see my husband. This was a Tuesday night, and I was informed that family visitation was on Mondays, that I could see him next Monday. I could not believe it! I said, "Who runs this place?" When they responded that it was the district attorney, I asked to see the district attorney. I was told that it was late and he had already gone home. I insisted on seeing the boss in charge, and two police officers walked me across the street to the district attorney's office. The district attorney did come from his home in River Oaks to talk to me, and I asked what the charges were against my husband. I was told that he had several unpaid traffic tickets that gave them the right to pick him up, but that he was suspected of heading a white collar crime ring involving lots of "money deals" in the Houston area.

I told the district attorney that if he was guilty, they could keep him – and that I strongly suspected that my husband was guilty, but I doubted that he would ever be convicted. I told the district attorney that my husband had an IQ of 180 and that I had come to realize that he had lived on the edge ever since I had first met and married him. I had always believed in him and had always tried to trust in him. Now, however, I was at the end of my rope and I did not believe that he would ever change. I had never visited a jail, much less had someone I cared about in it. The bail for his release was several thousand dollars that I did not have, so I asked the district attorney to allow me to see him, promising that I would not get the money for bail from my dad if I thought my husband was guilty. I said he could rot there.

What I saw when they brought him out was the devastation of a life that could have been great, the destruction of our marriage, and the living death of a father to a child. I saw twenty years of misery and courage and failure all mixed together, and realized that the ONLY things I had to show for twenty years of hell on earth was our beautiful daughter and what God had made of me using His potter's hands. This would have to be enough – and it was. I knew in my heart that my husband was guilty. All he wanted from me was a cigarette and for me to get him out of jail.

This really was the end, though I did see him one more time before he died in 1992.

When I returned home from that visit to the jail, Camille said, "Mom, why don't we get a divorce?" When a fourteen-year-old girl is wiser than her mom, it is time to take another look. I called my older brother that night and asked for the name of his friend who was an attorney in Houston. My brother called his attorney friend that night, and divorce proceedings were started immediately. The next day, I discovered that my husband had somehow managed to get into my bank account that I kept separate from his because of his irresponsibility, and that all my money was gone. Checks used to pay our essential bills like rent, water, electricity, and so forth were bouncing, so I still had to borrow money from my dad even though I did not pay bail money.

I felt like the storm was finally over, but I knew it wasn't the end of the consequences, because those continued, as they did for the Old Testament character David. I needed

73

my dad's help to pay off my personal debts, and I had to file bankruptcy in relation to the other debts that my husband had accrued without my knowledge. I continue to see the pain in my daughter; she's a wonderful, successful attorney, and wonderful person, but as a mother I can see the pain that she suffered all those years.

At that point in my life it dawned on me that many of the things that I feared the most had happened to me. I was broke, broken, divorced, and devastated. But with God's help, I had survived. In my early adult life, I feared having a husband who was unfaithful, being embarrassed and written about in the news, being without enough money to pay medical and drug bills, and having a husband who committed a crime and went to jail. I feared being embarrassed and exploited in the newspaper, and that had happened more than once. I feared being unable to pay my bills, and I had been there. No, I had LIVED there. I had even lived in a trailer when it took almost my entire teaching salary to pay for Camille's doctor and drug bills.

Yet, from the ashes of my life, the Lord began to rebuild. There were many things for which I could give thanks. I had a beautiful, intelligent daughter and knew if this was all I had that the pain had been worth it. There were other good things, too. God had molded and made me into a new person who was learning to depend not on what she could do but on what He could do, and even what He had already done – one who was learning in whatever circumstance I found myself to be content." Finally, I had acquired the wisdom to know the difference.

My career was flourishing, so I figured that the road ahead would be brighter, if perhaps somewhat lonelier. But that was before I met Dr. Frank Eggleston, my Sunday school teacher. A whole new life filled with hope and promise was about to begin.

Sara Eggleston

Part III

Living By Faith

Sara Eggleston

CHAPTER 5

A Bold Spirit

In December 1981, my future husband, Dr. Frank Eggleston, had prayed a prayer of relinquishment. Having never married and already thirty-nine years old, he prayed, "Lord, if you want me to be single for the rest of my life, I accept that. Whatever You want. I was hoping to find a Christian woman, but if it is Your will that I stay single, that's okay."

The rest of the story began a few weeks later – specifically, when I walked into his Sunday school class the first week of January, 1982. This is how he recalls it: "I was teaching Romans in Sunday school, and this gorgeous redhead walked into my class. I couldn't believe it – my mouth fell open. She walked in and she held her Bible upside down, and I wondered why it was upside down, but, oh my goodness, here she appeared like a gift from God."

Well, I don't know that I had my Bible upside down, but I guess I knew the passage that he was teaching on that day inside out.

At that time I'd been divorced about a year, and I'd been out with some guys who were not appropriate at all. My friend Millie had told me about Frank. We were looking through the church directory to see if there might be somebody there who might be a good match for me. "That's my husband's dentist," she said, when we came to Frank's photo.

"Ask him for me, please," I said. Well, Millie was going to talk with her husband and then tell me what she'd found out about Frank the next Sunday in church. When Millie sat down beside me, she said, "I found out that Frank is a really good dentist. My husband says that he washes his hands (this was before latex gloves) every time before he looks in your mouth!"

"Good grief," I said. "That's not what I needed to know! I'm going to have to find out about him myself!"

I had been dating a Christian psychologist who called and told me that there was a class on "self esteem" and that I should announce it to the singles' class. But I called Frank and asked him to announce this on Wednesday night. "Why don't you announce it yourself?" he suggested.

"Well," I replied, "I'm not going to be there this Wednesday because my daughter, Camille, is going to be one of the lead singers in the play *Oklahoma!* and I am going to be carpooling that evening. But," I paused, wondering how he might take what I was about to say, "I would really like to go to that seminar."

"So," he said. "Why don't you go?"

And he says I asked him out, but what I really said was, "Well, I don't know how to get there. I don't know where it is."

And he said, "But you just told me it's at Bammel Church."

"Yes, that's true," I replied. "But I don't know how to get there."

"Oh . . . oh . . . oh!" he said. "Could I pick you up?"

One of my friends was very disturbed at my dating practices, so he went next door, where an orthodontist lived, to ask about Frank. We were all trying to check him out. And the orthodontist said, "Oh, my goodness. Surely she's not going to go out with 'hands' Eggleston!" He paused, for effect, then laughed before continuing. "I'm just kidding," he said. "Frank is one of the nicest guys in the world. We're very good friends. He was in my wedding. Your friend will have a wonderful time."

Frank lived way across town from where I lived. And we both are very punctual – or, I should say, I am very punctual and Frank is EXTREMELY punctual. If he's not thirty minutes early, he thinks he's late. But that first time, I was still on the phone with my neighbor hearing what the orthodontist had said about Frank, when the doorbell rang. I wasn't dressed yet. I didn't have my shoes on. I didn't have parts of my clothing ensemble on yet, but I was dressed enough so I could answer the door, and I did that, apologizing for running late. Evidently, my lateness bothered me more than it bothered him since he just smiled and said something . . . something I don't remember because butterflies were setting in. It was probably something like, "Don't worry. I'm early. I'm usually early." And I probably said, "Well, I'm not usually late. In fact, I make it my goal to never be late."

The situation was further complicated by the fact that while I was getting dressed I had gotten a call that the topic of the seminar had been changed from self-esteem to single parenting. Evidently a lot of the expected attendees, mostly mothers raising their kids alone, were having trouble with their children, so the topic had been changed.

So as I'm finishing dressing, I'm thinking: *Here I am, going out with a guy who's never been married, and I'm late. I've practically asked him out. And we're going across town to a seminar that has no application to him whatsoever. How am I ever going to tell him that I really have messed up here?*

I waited until we got to about five miles from the destination until mentioning the change. "Uh . . . uh," I stammered. "I have something that I have to tell you. The uh, the uh . . . seminar's topic has been changed from esteem to single parenting. I know you don't have any children. Just pretend that you've got four boys and you're having trouble with all of them. And you can pretend that I'm the principal of the school and we're on these problems together. How does that sound?"

"Sounds okay to me," Frank replied.

Well, when we got to the seminar, it was as if Frank had had two-hundred forty-nine girlfriends before me, and most of them were there. "Frank, we didn't know you had any children . . . tee, hee, hee," they said. They were really teasing him. We went into the chapel. Frank was nursing a Dr. Pepper, which he loved to drink then, but doesn't anymore, because we don't do liquid sugar anymore. He kept setting his Dr. Pepper can on the floor and looking across at my legs. And I thought: *Oh my word. He is looking at my legs. I can't believe it.*

So I wrote on the edge of the notes he was taking, "Let's go out for dinner." I figured we might as well go out, since we weren't paying any attention to the seminar; we were too interested in each other. But I learned right then that he doesn't like anything written on his papers, because he got me a clean sheet, and I had to write it out again.

He nodded. And then he took me to dinner at Ouisie's restaurant, which is where he also asked me to marry him later on. The problem was that when we arrived, there was an ear, nose, and throat doctor and an endodontist in there, talking. They grabbed my date, and set me over in a window seat (we had an hour wait); then the three of them talked about root canals. And I thought: *Well, this has been a very interesting evening. First I ask him out to a seminar that has nothing whatsoever to do with him and his needs, and then he takes me out for dinner and dumps me here in the corner so he can chit chat with his friends!*

Of course, the other two weren't used to thinking of Frank as being connected with anybody, but when they realized their mistake they sent strawberries over to the table to say they were sorry for taking my date away. When we got up at the end of our dinner to go thank them, they were gone. So we just walked out the door. And I thought: *I've had a lovely evening, but he didn't pay for our dinner! I wonder if I ate so much that he doesn't have enough money to pay.*

I figured that maybe he knew the concierge and he just had a tab there. Then I thought: *No way. He's the kind of guy who checks every single line of the bill, and then tips exactly 15 percent – not estimated, but exactly. You know what, he just forgot to pay the bill!*

When he dropped me off, he kissed my hand. He didn't even try to kiss my lips – and I thought: *Well, um? How about that. A scholar and a gentleman. How nice.*

On his way home, Frank realized what had happened. The fact was that he was so distracted that he just forgot to pay the bill. We had gone looking for the other doctors to thank, and when we hadn't found them, we had just walked out. So he went back to Ouisie's and took care of it, with a little laughter thrown in with the tip.

The next morning he called me and asked, "Do you know what I did?"

And I said, "Yes, you didn't pay the bill, and I was so worried about it."

"I'm sorry. I just got distracted," he said (not admitting that he was distracted by being with me). "Would you go out again with me tonight?"

I gulped, but reality was reality. I already had a date with someone else that night. It took us awhile to work it all out, but within a very short time neither of us dated anyone else.

A couple of weeks later he took me to the home of Dr. Bill and Bea Roberts, who had told Frank that he could not be president of Houston District Dental Society without a first lady. At that party we discovered that Frank's cousin's daughter had been my college roommate. What a coincidence! (Of course, there are no coincidences with God.)

A short time after we met, I took Frank to visit my parents and also my brothers. I wanted to get their input about him, since I had made such a mess of things the first time around. On the way, Frank asked me if there was anything that he shouldn't talk about.

"Well," I said, "I have a father and one brother who are Democrats, and two brothers who are Republicans. Since you're a Republican, it would be really good not to mention politics, because if you happen to join the family later on, you would break the tie, and that would NOT be popular when we're going to the farm to see my dad and mom."

"Okay," Frank nodded. "No politics."

"There's another thing," I added. "After we've been there about five minutes, Daddy is going to say, 'I don't guess y'all would want to go over to the ranch, would you?' You will think it's impolite to my mom to get up and leave so soon after arriving, because you're very polite to women, but Mother knows Daddy and that he wants to show you around, so it's just fine with her."

Well, just as I'd predicted, after we'd been there about five minutes, Daddy said "I don't guess y'all would want to go over to the ranch, would you?"

When we got to the ranch, Daddy was surprised that Frank knew how to open and shut the gates. "Where did you learn that, son?" he asked.

"On a dude ranch," Frank replied.

I thought Daddy was going to fall down on the ground and roll around, overcome with laughter. "A DUDE ranch, son?" he asked, when he had regained his composure. "Why not a real ranch, like this one? There's plenty of real ranches in Texas where you wouldn't have to pay to learn how to open and shut the gates!"

"Well, sir," Frank replied with a little twinkle in his eye. "At the time, I didn't know anybody who owned a farm. I'm a city fella with a lot of different interests, but there's no place in the city where you can learn to open and shut gates like these here."

On Memorial weekend Frank asked me to marry him, in a roundabout sort of way. There had been a robbery close to my home, so I wanted to have some of my jewelry appraised. We had a date for Saturday night, and I told him on Friday that I was going to have some jewelry appraised the next day, and I wondered if he would want to go with me.

"I certainly don't!" he said. And he wasn't polite about it, which isn't like Frank at all. "I certainly do not want to go to *any* jewelry store."

"Fine," I replied. "But we still have a date Saturday night, right?"

"Yes."

"Well, I'll see you then."

He called me back in a little while and said, "Sara, I've been taken to the jewelry store and the furniture store by about two hundred women. That's why I'm not interested in going to pick out any kind of jewelry."

And I said, "I'm not picking out jewelry; I'm going to have my jewelry appraised. I'll see you Saturday night."

And he said, "No, I am going to come. I'll take you.

What time do you want to go?"

So we got in the car to drove to the jewelry store and he said, "Sara, what kind of ring do you want?"

And I thought: *He hasn't even asked me to marry him yet.* "Are you talking about an *engagement* ring?"

And he said, "Yes."

"Well, I have a lot of jewelry," I said. "But I don't have to have a diamond ring. I don't care what kind of ring I have, if that is what you're talking about. I didn't realize that this was in the works yet. But since you're asking, what kind of ring did you want to buy?"

And he said, "About a car's worth."

And I said, "What kind of car? A Mercedes or a Volkswagen?"

And he said, "About an Oldsmobile's worth."

And I said, "Oh, that's pretty good."

So we got to the jewelry store and I had my jewelry appraised while he went over and looked at diamonds. He picked out loose diamonds and had three of them put out on the little velvet pad. "These are the three I can afford," he said. "Which one do you like?"

So I chose the one I liked best, and I still love it to this day.

Next, we were going to take Frank's mother shopping and then to lunch.

He said, "Let's go get my mom, and we'll take her shopping." Then he said, "Excuse me, I need to go to the bathroom." Well, Frank is like most men – he doesn't go to the bathroom very often because he doesn't drink enough water, and it was totally unlike him to have to make an emergency visit, so I figured something was up.

Then we got to his mom's house, and again he said, "Excuse me, I've got to go to the bathroom."

When we got to Foley's, again he said, "Excuse me, I've got to go to the bathroom."

Finally I said, "Frank, are you sick?"

I later learned that he was excusing himself so he could call to transfer money to pay for the ring, making sure that the jewelry store could have it ready by that night, making reservations at Ouisie's, where we'd had our first date, and so forth. His plan was to take me there so he could ask me to marry him, and he was making sure everything was in order.

He told me to wear what I wore on our first date, so I did. He took me to Ouisie's and we sat at the very same table again, and he asked me to marry him.

And I said, "Oh, really. You want to marry me? Ask me again." So he asked me twice. Then, when I accepted his offer, he said, "Sara, you're not going to have a ring. Is that all right?"

I said, "That's okay. I don't care. As long as I have you."

"Are you sure it's all right?" he continued. "When you get to Sunday school in the morning you won't have anything to show around."

"No, no," I said. "It's no problem."

After supper he took me by his house and said, "I've got to call your father and ask his permission." It was humorous because just that morning we had talked to Dad and Mom, and my brother was there and he had said, "Sissy, when are you going to ask this guy to marry you?"

And I had said, "Well, this one has to ask me."

Frank got my dad on the phone and asked Daddy's permission to marry me. And then Frank said, "Let me talk to Joe." And he said to Joe, "Joe, she finally asked me. We're going to get married."

Then we went into the living room and he put on "our" song – from *Cats*, a song called "Memory." There were flowers and candles, and then Frank said, "Excuse me, I've got to go to the bathroom." Of course, that was where he had been hiding the ring, which I didn't know he had because he had made it all happen so fast. And we told Camille, who was thrilled.

I asked Frank when he wanted to get married. "I have three weeks off in the summer. That would be the best time," I said.

Speaking of fast, what I was suggesting was just another six weeks away. Then Frank started hyperventilating. I thought: *I'm not really sure this guy wants to get married. He doesn't realize that I have to get a whole school together in six weeks. Maybe I should find him a paper bag.*

He didn't tell me until years later that he thought that six weeks was not enough time for me to get a wedding together. "How about September?" he suggested.

Then I thought: *This guy has no clue as to what I do. I've got a thousand kids, eighty teachers, I have to do report cards (I made it my practice to read all the children's report cards and to write personal notes on them, to encourage them). I can't get married until after the first report cards go out.*

So I said, according to Frank (if he's right, I must have been pretty nervous), "I think I can fit you in after the first report cards."

So our anniversary is September 25, after the first report cards went out that year. We only had a little weekend honeymoon in San Antonio, but we've really had an ongoing honeymoon ever since . . . in very many wonderful, wonderful places.

In 1982, right after we married, the winter was very cold, and we went up to Munday. Daddy had gotten Frank some insulated coveralls, the importance of which Frank did not realize until all the men – Frank, my brothers, and my father – were outside in eleven degree weather doing chores on the ranch. Since Frank was more or less ignorant in terms of typical ranch chores, Daddy tried to find him something to do. "See that pond over there, that's iced over?" he said, pointing toward a bunch of cattle that were standing on the ice. When Frank nodded, Daddy continued, "Go on over and punch a hole in that ice so the cattle can get to the water."

Frank's initial issue, as a scientist, was to wonder if the cattle were smart enough to know that they couldn't fall through, or just dumb enough that it didn't make any difference. In any case, he started at a place where there was still running water, and tried to open that up. When Daddy saw what Frank was doing, he yelled, "No, no, no! Not there! They can get to that already. Go out where the ice is thick and do it."

"How big a hole do you want?" Frank asked.

"About the size of a number three washtub," Daddy replied.

Well, Frank being the precise person that he is, said,

"I'm sorry, sir, but I don't know how big a number three washtub is."

"I thought you had some letters after your name," Daddy chided.

"Yes, sir. That's true. But my degree is in teeth, not in ice."

And Daddy laughed and went out and punched the hole through, himself.

My brothers, who were witnessing the whole thing, said later, "Daddy yelled at Frank, just like he yells at us. That makes him part of the family!"

Some time later, Frank and I went into a hardware store where he had shopped since he was a child, and right up there on the wall behind the counter were five washtubs, numbered zero, one, two, three, and four. All along we had been using a number four tub to wash our ferns. So we all got to laugh again when we told my folks about that. There is a principle that we use, which is, "You see what you know." Frank never saw the number three washtub because he did not know about number three washtubs.

In 1981, I had become principal at Memorial Parkway Elementary, which was a regular, average school, and I began learning how to discern, evaluate, and diagnose the teaching "act." I was able to go into classrooms at the invitation of the teachers and work with them to help their children learn. I was able to figure out what was wrong – if the teacher was not using proper feeling tone, if she wasn't asking questions – whatever. Together, we diagnosed the problem. It was amazing what happened in that school.

I asked the teachers if they wanted to learn how to become more effective teachers, and they all said they did. Of course, they were already overworked – a school of more than a thousand children and a staff of ninety-two. It was difficult for me – I was still really young, and a lot of the teachers were much older than I was – to be the boss, and to come into a school where I had been an assistant principal (an assistant principal is a friend to the teachers) and have the authority to hire and fire and all the rest. I've always felt that bosses have more power than they need to have, because they hold the person's life in their hands. Anyone with that kind of authority, if they know what they're doing, has more authority than they want. At least I knew that to be true for me.

I was a very forceful personality, and if a person was not effective enough and committed enough to want to learn how to teach children, if they could not teach my child or my grandchild, then I didn't want them in my school. If I did have to fire someone, I would do all I could to find them another position. But eventually every teacher on my team was someone I would have chosen to teach my own child. And they were the best, I thought, in the world.

Well, one day one of them came to talk with me, and she said, "We don't like these classes. We're having to stay after school. It's extra work and we're tired of learning all this stuff you're wanting us to learn."

I knew that she was speaking for the whole staff.

She said, "I'm tired."

So I said, "Well, you know, you agreed as a staff to do this, and we're only about halfway finished. I've been giving you a pre-test, and if you all know the material then I skip that and we go on to something else. I've been writing the curriculum as we go. What if I allow you to teach the next lesson if you can get a ninety-five on the next test? If you already know how to do all of that, then you can be excused."

"Okay," she said. And as she got to the door, I said, "Tell the rest of the staff this applies to them as well."

The next week she came back to me and said, "You got me, didn't you? You knew that you had to know the material in order to be able to teach it. I tried writing the next lesson, and I couldn't do it."

I still practice this principle today with people who are trying to teach others. The point is really simple: If you know the material well enough to apply it to your own life, then you know it well enough to pass it on to others in a way that it will benefit them, also.

So whether it's teaching, ministry, medicine, dentistry, sales, whatever it is – make it your goal to master the material and methods to the best of your ability, and then pass what you know along to trustworthy people who can teach others also. It's actually a biblical principle, which the apostle Paul expressed to his young pastoral protégé, Timothy, as recorded in 2 Timothy 2:2: "And the things that thou hast heard of me among many witnesses, the same commit thou to faithful men, who shall be able to teach others also." It's the principle of multiplication, which is the best way to have the greatest impact possible in any field of endeavor to which you feel called.

Sara Eggleston

CHAPTER 6

Keepsakes, Copiers, and the Teaching Moment

When Camille was twenty, she asked Frank to adopt her, which is amazing because we don't really know very many adults who are adopted by adults. But she wanted to change her name and to have him for her daddy. Frank had learned from the *Catholic Digest* that you build a relationship with the child; you don't just love the child because of the spouse. And that's what Frank had done – loved Camille not for my sake, but for who she is. In other words, he had built his own relationship with her, a wonderful and beautiful relationship – so much so that when she became a mother, she named her first son after him.

Of course, every relationship, especially one between a parent and child that begins when the child is older than an infant, can have its humps and bumps. For example, one day when Camille was still a teenager, she was sitting in the corner and Frank just up and asked, "Camille, what do you know about sex?"

"Mother," she implored me. "Make him leave me alone!"

And she threw her books down and blasted up the stairs. Frank and I had each been sitting in the room, working. So when Camille was out of earshot, I said to Frank, "Honey, I'd love for you to explain sex to me. I mean, a guy who had all those dates before me and a degree in biology – I'm sure you can enlighten me. I would just love to hear your explanation."

Well, I guess he wasn't as prepared to discuss that subject as he had sounded when he put the question to Camille. He just shook his head and went back to his work. So I never got to hear his take on sex.

Very shortly after that, in the summertime, I went to a Mamie McCullough seminar for principals. I was so honored to get chosen to attend. I just love Mamie and Zig Ziglar. We became personal friends with them after that. And Mamie just absolutely loved what I was doing.

While I was gone to that seminar, Camille was dating a certain young man who had wrecked three Audis despite the fact that he did not drink. He made sure that I understood that he was a good Baptist and he never drank a drop. So I told Frank, "You know, this young man is more dangerous sober than most of them are drunk. I wish he would drink a little bit. I pray for Camille's safety every time she goes out with him. I'm scared to death that he's going to wreck the car with her in it."

While I was attending that seminar, Camille broke up with the fellow. Frank came down the stairs and found the pizza left uneaten, the boyfriend gone, and Camille gone upstairs to cry. The scenario was outside Frank's personal experience. So he called me and asked, "What am I going to do with her?"

"I don't know," I replied, not hiding my sense of relief. "You'll think of something. You can handle it. Just handle it."

So Frank started from what he knew. "Now what I did when I quit girlfriends," he told her, "I just boxed up all the stuff that belonged to them and gave back what was theirs. And if there was other stuff – you know, memorabilia of any kind – I boxed that up and put it in the attic. So, let's decide what you're going to keep, and box it up, and put it in the attic." They did it together, and he was thrilled to help.

One thing that was a challenge after we married was how to combine households. Frank had this Navy table with a glass top and the Navy wheel showing through from the bottom. He wanted to put that table in the living area in the vicinity of my white velvet couch. They didn't quite match, but I decided that if it was that important to him, it didn't really matter what the living room looked like. So we did put it in there, though I did later move it, saying that one day he could build me a house and we would build one room around that Navy table. So that table is in our den today with other things in a nautical motif, with colors to match.

Frank had a variety of personal keepsakes that needed new homes, including "Oscar the Skull." As a dentist, Frank had a lot of teeth models secreted about here and there, but I told him that Oscar could not live in my house; he had to go to the dental office. Today they use synthetic skulls for demonstration purposes, but Oscar was a real human. I was afraid that if I let Oscar stay, I might end up someday holding that skull in my hand, like Shakespeare's Hamlet held the skull of his former friend, the court jester, Yorick, and said, "Alas, poor Yorick. I knew him. . . ."

Frank also had this one little plaque that had written upon it the words, from Galatians, "Bear ye one another's' burdens." A former girlfriend had given this to him, so I put that in the laundry room, where it just seemed to fit quite well, all things considered. When Camille went off to college the following year, I sent it with her. I thought it would be good for her to learn to bear other people's burdens, and that little plaque would be a good reminder.

Since we were still attending the same church where we'd met, and where Frank had been teaching the singles' class for some time, after we married, I suggested that we should participate in an age-appropriate group, since we were nearly forty years old.

"I think we should be with people our age," I said.

"Sweetheart," he replied, "I want to attend the 'young marrieds' class."

"You've got to be kidding," I said. "Some of those kids are twenty years old. We're old enough to be their parents!"

"No," he said, "we have to go there. We'll go just one Sunday."

Well, we visited that one Sunday, and before long Frank became one of the teachers of that class, and twelve years later we were still in that class. One Sunday he was teaching, and explaining how we put our households together, and how things that he'd had just seemed to disappear, and he said to me, right in front of the class, "Sara, there was this one thing that I really did like. It was a little plaque that said 'Bear ye one another's burdens.' What happened to that plaque?"

And I replied, "I can't believe you asked me that in front of the whole class! That was from a former girlfriend, and now it's at college with Camille." Well, of course, they all just cracked up about that.

Another thing that we had to work through when we first married was that with Frank's birthday being December 4, he often got both birthday and Christmas gifts together at the same time. All his life he had heard, "Here is your birthday present, Frank. And while we're on the subject, here's your Christmas present, too."

To try to keep things a little bit separate, his mother never put up the Christmas tree until after his birthday. Well, when you're a school principal, you put up the Christmas tree on Thanksgiving weekend, say Friday or Saturday, because it's the only time you have a long weekend between then and Christmas, and after work during that same period, it's nonstop activity of one kind or another.

Our first Thanksgiving, I tried to explain to him that I couldn't put up the Christmas tree until Christmas if I didn't do it during Thanksgiving weekend. But he insisted that his mother's tradition was his preference. Since I could see how important it was to him, I tried to make it work – but now we put up the Christmas tree soon after Halloween, even though I'm no longer in education, because we still seem to have so very much to do between one holiday and the next.

The actual solution to this dilemma was to celebrate Frank's birthday at another time. Since I knew he loved July 4, one day I said, "Sweetheart, let's just have your birthday party on July 4, and make it your new birthday."

So the grandchildren ask today, "Nana, why does Poppa get two birthdays?"

"Because he can," I say. "And because he wants to." I'm just waiting for the day when all three of them request their own second birthdays.

Frank has been the president of many dental organizations since we married, which is one reason I like to say that more people have seen me eat chicken at the head table than any woman alive. Once when we were having a dental organization meal at the Houstonian, a very famous columnist who was our speaker that night was sitting at the head table, and I was running late. I had taken clothes to change into, something a little more dressy than a principal's outfit. But after school a child had fallen on their bike, right outside my door. The child was bleeding – I don't do blood or shots; I'm terrified of shots, which is why I became a teacher instead of a nurse, since those were the only two choices you had when I was growing up. Nonetheless, I had doctored the child up a bit, getting blood on my skirt, and I was trying to slip in unnoticed.

But when Frank saw me come in, he announced, "Oh, there she is – coming in right now!" So everybody turned and looked at me. There was no way I could do my imitation of Miss America, and there was nobody to sing that "There she is, Miss America" song. Frankly, I was mortified, so I just made my way over and sat down next to this world-renowned columnist, who then started talking about the failures, horrors, and sins of public education.

Of course, the table was very, very quiet. It was amazing. Finally, I interrupted him and said, "Sir, the reason no one is responding is that you are our guest, and we're so happy and proud to have you as our speaker, and we enjoy reading your column. But everyone here knows that I am a principal at a public elementary school (and this blood on my skirt is from a child who got hurt and needed my help, which is why I was late). I assure you that I don't have the kind of school you're describing, at all. In fact, it's one of the best in the nation."

Well, I expect our speaker learned a lesson that night, and so did I – be sure you know your audience before you start in on what might be a popular topic elsewhere, or you might get some egg on your face, accented with chicken grease on your shirt.

Another great lesson that I learned during this time occurred in a similar setting in Katy, Texas, where I and a number of other principals from the area had been invited to view a play that had been written by one of our peers, a principal from Katy. The play was set right there in Katy. In this case, the master of ceremonies gave the introduction, in which he talked about the playwright and how talented she was. Since the woman was a very good friend of mine, whom I had brought to the Katy school district, I didn't feel jealous of her success at all. In fact, I've always tried to just enjoy and celebrate and be grateful for the successes of others – to be happy for them and not threatened at all – because during my own years of misery and horror and fear, I had learned that if I didn't share in other people's joy, when I had none of my own, I would have very little joy in my life over the long haul.

The master of ceremonies went on and on about how wonderful this woman was, and he seemed to speak of her as if she were the greatest principal in the world. Well, all ten of the rest of the principals, including me, were sitting there, listening to him go on and on. Finally, one of the guys turned to me and said, "Well what are we, dog poop?" Obviously, he was upset that the master of ceremonies had made so much of the other principal, and all because she had produced a play about the little town of Katy without acknowledging the rest of us.

About a week later we attended another ceremony, this one in Dallas, and sponsored by the Baylor College of Dentistry honoring Frank as alumnus of the year. And, of course, throughout the evening there were many wonderful things said about Frank, all of them true and well-deserved. But when the dean spoke, he said, "We're all here tonight to honor one man. And we're so proud of Dr. Frank Eggleston." He listed many of Frank's accolades, and then he said, "But, you know, Frank would be the first to say that you are the ones who are important." Then he described the audience – the rest of us, and how we had supported the college of dentistry, and given of our time and energy and money. He went on and on and on, similar to the way that master of ceremonies had done a week earlier, but in this case everyone felt like a million dollars.

I thought: *Wow! Wow! I'll give them some more money if I've got any. This is just great.*

So when I go out speaking, I treasure the privilege of the platform, and try to keep in mind how our words can lift people up. If we are careful about what we say and how we say it, even if the words don't come out exactly the way we had hoped, we can still build people up without having anyone else feel torn down.

When I was principal of Memorial Parkway Elementary, there was a priest who met in our school with people from his church. Father Tim weighed about three hundred pounds, and I absolutely adored him. They had no place to store the communion wine, so without telling me, he put it in the gym closet. Keep in mind that in Texas you cannot have firearms, drugs, or alcohol on school property. Well, one day in the summertime, when school was out, I happened to open the door to that closet in the gym. There were cases and cases of wine, all stacked neatly and all right there in plain sight.

I called Father Tim right away and said, "Father Tim, I thought you loved me! Are you trying to get me fired?"

"Oh no, ma'am," he said. "What is it?"

"You can't store your communion wine on school property. It's against the law."

"But it's for the church," he replied.

"It doesn't matter," I said. "I could have gotten in bad

trouble, even if I didn't know it was there. But now that I do know, I need for you to come and get this right now and take it to your house." He came and I helped him load it into his vehicle, hoping all the while that he would not have a heart attack from over-exertion. All I needed was a priest in cardiac arrest surrounded by cases of wine in my school's gymnasium!

I also had an attempted kidnapping in that school, which was amazing, and it influenced my life as a principal. I asked that the parents sign the children out, because you never know in a school that size what might happen. Usually kids are kidnapped by an estranged parent. So I had to have the signature whenever anyone came by to pick up one of the children. In this case, I had gotten a call from an aunt, saying that whichever parent was not supposed to have the child was coming to take the child out of school. So I hid the child under my desk until the police could get there to help.

About the same time, I had three FBI agents show up one day, without any advance notice, wanting a private audience with me. They were in their suits. They said that they had found me in the database as a person who had been in a witness protection program. They were rather arrogant and pompous, and they made it clear that theirs was an important job. I was sitting behind my desk, since there was no other place to sit – I normally did not put a desk between me and my audience, but thought it would be a good idea with three of them ganging up on me.

"How can I help you?" I asked.

"Well," they said. "We need you to enroll a student in

your school whose family is under protective custody. Most people who are in the witness protection program end up in mental institutions. Very few are emotionally stable. Since you are a principal, we need to know: Are you emotionally stable?"

I was just a little bit insulted, so I said, "What day is it? There are days when I don't feel emotionally stable at all. I'll bet your wives have that problem, too. I can't believe this question. If you weren't FBI, I would consider it arrogant. But I would also wonder about your IQs. What is it that you guys really need from me?" Then they laughed. So did I, though I didn't forget it for a long time.

One day I took Frank to see the school. When we walked in, he looked at the plaque on the wall and said, "That's my cousin, Dr. Bob Field, a veterinarian, who is on the school board." That was certainly a surprise to me.

At that time we had an extra custodian on our staff, named Pablo. When I took Frank in and introduced him to the teachers and custodians, Pablo said, "Whoooo. Missy got her a young one!"

"I'll have you know he is several months older than I am," I said. I was just infuriated. The very idea!

And Pablo said, "Whooo. He's a nice man!"

Pablo was reassigned the next week, but I really had nothing to do with that, I promise.

Shortly thereafter, Frank wanted to go out to the school and use my copier. I had some work to do on a Sunday afternoon, so I told him I would be doing my paperwork and he could use the copier. I bought a ream of paper, because we couldn't use the school's paper for our own personal use without helping to pay the costs. So I put money in the petty cash fund, gave him a ream of paper, went into the office and did my work, and came back about an hour later, and it looked like a paper bomb had gone off in there.

This was a new copier, in a new and beautifully designed room, which had won a design award for being one of the best in the nation – gorgeous. And the whole room was like snow had fallen, in eight and a half by eleven inch flakes. There were sheets of paper everywhere.

I said, "What have you done?"

He said, "There are specks on this copier."

I said, "Frank, that is a brand new machine. Specks? Specks on a paper are not the same thing as specks on a tooth."

And he said, "Oh, yes they are!"

And I said, "We don't have time for this. You can just go to Kinko's. The very idea!"

He said, "Oh, come now. You're just defending your school's honor."

I laughed, and then said, teasingly, "You are banned from the school except for social events."

After ten years at that school I was asked by the school board to move to Pattison. I really didn't want to because we had just married and had a teenage daughter, and I would have to open the new school in the same school year in which I was still principal of another school – in effect, run two schools at the same time, on the same money. But the third time they asked me, I agreed, and it was one of the smartest moves I ever made.

One father, an alcoholic, came to see me, crying, because I was leaving Memorial Parkway Elementary. He was so sweet. Once his boys had stolen a bicycle, and I had been furious with him. "What are you doing?" I had asked. "Sitting down and reading your newspaper, drinking, not supervising those boys? You cannot let them go out the upstairs window and go steal things in the neighborhood while you're sitting there in the house!"

He nodded sheepishly, as I continued, "I want you to get in an AA program, and get yourself straightened out so you can take care of these boys." And, amazingly, he did that.

When I was leaving, he thanked me. "It was because you intervened in our lives that we're still together today," he said. "It saved my marriage and my kids."

I prefer to think that the fellow did the changing, but that God did the saving by intervening, using me.

When I think back to my time at Memorial Parkway, many incidents come to mind, one somewhat humorous. We had a "gifted" program at that school, offering kids with higher IQ special classes that allowed them to do things that other children were not allowed to do. For example, we had the first computers in the district because we had a very gifted teacher who had taught computer science in New Jersey – so we had some really good programs. But the gifted children were sometimes arrogant and not very nice in the way they spoke to or treated the other children who were not in the gifted program.

Some boys who were not in the gifted program got hold of some chocolate ex-lax® and gave it to the gifted boys, which of course made them have to go to the bathroom quite a lot. Now I actually thought it was very funny, and that the gifted boys had gotten exactly what they needed and deserved, but I had to discipline the others. So I brought them into my office, and I asked them where they got the chocolate ex-lax®. They admitted that they had stolen it from Randall's. So I told them they had to go to Randall's, talk to the police officer there, and pay for what they'd stolen. I got their mothers to help me. We drove down to the grocery store, talked to the officer there, and they were able to pay for what they had stolen. That was their lesson. Of course I admonished them, even though they thought it was funny, to not do this anymore.

Then I called in the gifted boys and encouraged them to not take candy from other people. I asked, "Why do you think they might have given you the chocolate ex-lax® as a joke? Do you think that you've been acting in an arrogant way?" I recited some of the things I remembered them doing and saying that were arrogant and rude, and I tried to help them learn an important lesson, that when you treat people in such a manner, you won't end up with very many friends.

Well, the mothers of the gifted boys did not think I had punished the other boys enough. But I told them it was my school, and that this was the way it was going to be. I said, "You should try to teach your boys something about humility, because it certainly was humiliating for them to have to run to the bathroom all the time – but it didn't hurt them. Hopefully they've learned a good lesson through this experience."

The parents at Nottingham Country Elementary, which

was a sister school to Pattison Elementary, had petitioned
the school board for me to become the principal of their
new school. The reason they wanted me was because I had
a track record for having the highest test scores in the district. I went over to the school and evaluated, noting that
mothers were going into and out of the classrooms with
some regularity, but without any educational reason to do
so. The mothers were interrupting instruction and interfering with the "teaching moment" that I had studied in
great detail through the years under Dr. Madeline Hunter
from California. When a child is about to "get it," you don't
want a mother walking into the classroom just to give her
child a kiss, even though mothers can be helpful on the
campus *if they have specific jobs to do – jobs that do not inter-
fere with the teaching moment.* In effect, their doting attempts
at encouragement were actually interfering with their children's educational progress.

So before I accepted the principal position at Pattison,
we had a meeting with the parents, and I asked them why
they wanted me as their principal. "Honestly," was their
reply, "we just want our kids to have higher scores. We
want them to be able to go to the best colleges and univer-
sities. We know that it all starts in elementary school, and
we think that you know how to get that job done."

"I am willing to try, if you are willing to do the things
that I ask," I said. I wrote on the chalkboard: "Teaching moment – instruction will not be interrupted." Then I added,
"There will be jobs. I would love to have any of you up
there any time, but you will not go into the classrooms and
interrupt instruction; I don't and you don't either, if you

want the scores to come up. Secondly, you will check your child out at the front office. I told them about the attempted kidnapping I'd experienced earlier. I have to know who's going where and with whom. And you have to check them out. You can't just go get them whenever you please, especially during instruction time, because that will not be allowed, except in emergency. We're here to teach your kids and to help them learn how to learn. This cannot be accomplished in little bits and pieces or disjointed segments. There needs to be continuity, without disruption."

It was clear to me from their response that they were willing to work with me. So I added one more thing. "Third," I said, "I want them to learn to give. These children are gifted, smart, wealthy – this will be like a private school. And one of the most valuable things they can learn is to help those less privileged than they are. So we will find ways to help them become generous and kind, contributing citizens of our world, even while they are still young."

Part IV

Living In Victory

Sara Eggleston

CHAPTER 7

Married to the Dentist of the World – Serving the Creator of the World

In 1990, I attended a seminar for school principals that was held on Walt Disney property, incorporating many of those creative and positive things that Walt Disney did with property, and isolating principles that we could take back to our schools and implement with the parents' support.

By 1993, we had adopted "Flat Stanley" as our mascot, based on the character created by the late Jeff Brown in 1964, who could make himself flat so he could fit inside an envelope. We thus become very early participants in what is now an international literacy program called the "Flat Stanley Project." Flat Stanley can fit in an envelope or a book, so all the children made Flat Stanleys, and we had a map in the library that showed where Flat Stanley had gone. If their parents or grandparents traveled anywhere, Flat Stanley could go with them, and we could put a pin on the map that showed that he had visited Russia, Scandinavia, Germany, Austria, Switzerland, Australia, New Zealand, Hawaii, Maui, Indonesia, China – these parents traveled everywhere.

In 1994, Pattison Elementary won the National Award of Excellence, the highest award in the nation for excellence in education. This was a great achievement since almost always a ghetto-type school won this award. Pattison was a high-achieving school where most parents were professionals. We had to show compassion and progress in order to be eligible. I received the award for the school from President Clinton at the White House. Twelve Pattison moms paid their own way to go along, but only three people were allowed at the ceremony, so my gifted education teacher, the PTA president, and I attended the ceremony. Frank was "in charge" of the other Pattison moms, who loved him and called him the "First Man."

Every mom who went to Washington with us took her child's Flat Stanley along. He jumped off the Washington monument and met with senators and representatives when we visited Capitol Hill. The kids had made and given me a Flat Stanley that looked like me. So I took mine all dressed up to the ceremony. They had made one for Frank, too, and dressed his in playclothes. His Flat Stanley met Tipper Gore, the Vice President's wife, by the Washington Monument. Mrs. Gore had been jogging. When the moms saw her duck into a restroom, they all followed her in there and got photos. Mrs. Gore was very gracious and so were her secret service agents.

Every day during that trip, I would call the school and someone would hold the phone up to the intercom, so I could tell the children where Flat Stanley had been and what he'd been doing, and we just had so much fun!

The next year I was nominated by the staff and parents to represent Texas among the representative distinguished principals of all the states in America, and I won that – so once again I got to go to Washington, and I spoke from the White House grounds. The award was presented by Richard Riley, the US Secretary of Education. Each state representative made a little speech – it was a wonderful time – another wonderful time.

In fact, 1995 was a banner year for us in many ways. Our precious grand twins were born on June 1– Joshua King Hailey and Sara Elizabeth Hailey, each bearing part of Frank's name and part of mine, too.

In 1995, Frank served as President of the Texas Dental Association. He was in Austin and Washington eighty days that year, meaning eighty days out of his practice – and eighty days away from home. While I was proud and happy for him, it felt in some ways like we were the proverbial ships passing in the night.

That winter, Frank was named Texas Dentist of the Year. He was honored in the same room in the hotel in Austin where I had been named National Distinguished Principal the previous summer. We took the twins and their parents with them. I bought the twins' outfits from *The Wooden Soldier* magazine, a high-end clothing concern for children.

The outfits were matching, of course, black velvet with red trim. They were quite the picture, believe me.

In 1995, I asked Frank to build us a new home. I figured if he could be away from his practice eighty days and we did not go bankrupt, then we could afford a bigger house. Besides, we still needed the right kind of room to surround his precious Navy table, his one major heirloom from his days in the service.

So we purchased and demolished a darling little bungalow a block away from Frank's childhood home, where we lived for the year it took to build the new home. We celebrated the twins' first Christmas in Frank's childhood home and even used the Christmas tree that he'd had as a child – we found it intact in the attic. Frank's precious mom was in a nursing facility while all this was happening, in the final stages of Alzheimer's disease. We now suspect that her diet of butter, lard, white bread, cokes, ice cream, and processed foods must have exacerbated and accelerated the disease, which she suffered with (and Nancy Reagan called "the long good-bye") for her final thirteen years. Every day of that year was a mixture of happiness and sadness for Frank. I watched him carry it all with courage, sharing both the joy and the pain.

Mother Eggleston died the day we moved into our just-finished home, June 30, 1996. Her funeral was a celebration of the life of a wonderful woman who loved and trained her son to become all that he could be. Of the many humorous or touching stories we recall from those days, we remember "Mattress Mac" who came to fix all the beds in our new home to get ready for the guests who would be coming for the funeral. What a job he did! And then there was Camille and the teachers from my school coming to set up the bathrooms and kitchen. Everyone pitched in, and everything worked out.

Camille sang at the funeral – she has the voice of an angel. And Frank led us onward in faith, step by step. As an only child whose father had died when Frank was twenty-seven, he showed me, and has continued to show me, about trusting God because He is in charge, and accepting what we cannot change, while still striving for excellence.

Over the next two years, I had a couple of wrecks on the Katy Freeway going back and forth to school. One of the wrecks totaled Frank's Toronado – it was a three-car pileup and I was in the middle. I remember getting out of the car and being so thankful that nobody had been seriously injured. But the guys were all cussing and yelling at the woman, whose fault the accident was, and carrying on, so I just tried to calm everything down.

She didn't have a driver's license; she didn't have any insurance. I was trying to be kind, the wreckers were coming, and the traffic was wall to wall – a veritable Houston, Texas, rush hour disaster. Months later I was subpoenaed to be a witness for her. I went in there dressed like a principal, wondering why I had been subpoenaed. I mean, it seemed a bit outrageous that she wanted me to testify in her behalf when she had come across three lanes of traffic, run into me, totaled my car, and squished me into two other cars. Did she want me to say what a good job of driving she had been doing?

I told the judge, "She must be nuts. She ran into me and wrecked my car, and I'm supposed to testify for her?"

Well, the judge was furious. He threw his pencil, not at me, and then said to me, "You get on over here on the other side!"

The woman said, "But you were so nice to me."

I replied, "Well, I wasn't dead. Why should I have yelled at you; what was done was already done."

Another time, on Halloween, I was on my way home, and a police officer with three prostitutes in the back of his cruiser ran into the back of my car when I was sitting in bumper to bumper traffic. In my rearview mirror, I could see it coming, but I couldn't do anything about it. The women had their hands cuffed behind them, but there was no screen between them and the policeman. The women were butting him with their heads, just enough to make him turn to look in their direction for an instant . . . at just the wrong time.

My car was totaled, and this time my body was nearly totaled, too. My body was so jarred by the impact that my retinas detached soon after that. Many other bad things happened, as well.

For a long time I was confined to a wheelchair from the pain of my arthritis. Ultimately, Frank said, "You've done thirty years. It's time to come home and get well."

Since that accident, I've had laser surgery, cryo procedures, and thousands of stitches to try to hold my eyes together. But the retina in one eye was partially detached, so I was lying on my bed to help it reattach. I had to stay in one position so it would "stick" and heal – otherwise I was facing a "buckle" procedure to try and keep it in.

I ran my school that year from Thanksgiving until after Christmas from my bed at home. Then I had to be driven to school, so with Frank still practicing dentistry, the mothers signed up to come and get me – they loved it because it was an hour-long drive and they had my full attention in the car, one way, where they could tell me anything they wanted to tell me. And they said there was a waiting list. People loved coming to get me and bring me home. They said that they would drive out here and get me every day if I would just stay. And when I retired there were so many honors. There were many honors and flowers and lots of love. It is a good thing to leave when people still want you rather than having them say to each other, "I wonder when that old lady is going to retire?"

The rest of that year was one to forget. I was so sick. I was retired. I was in depression. I no longer had the children around me all the time, or their parents, or their teachers – many of whom had worked for me for sixteen years. I knew them better than I knew my own family – I was in every classroom every day, and I saw them all the time. We were all there, working together to make a difference in children's lives. I felt my life had purpose, that being a principal, helping children to learn, was my ministry. I had loved every minute of it. It was fun for me. I tried to make it fun for them, and I know I did, and I missed it.

In addition, I was so afraid I was going to go blind, and I couldn't walk. I was scooting around on my seat most of the time, and my knees were hurting. I was on Relafen, and

Sara Eggleston

Ultram, and had cortisone shots in every joint in my body. I used Vioxx (which was later taken off the market) and Celebrex – sometimes I felt like a walking, I should say, crawling, pharmacy.

From 1999 to 2003 Frank served on the American Dental Association Board of Trustees. As a result, we went to Chicago every other month for a week for those four years. Frank says it drives terror into a man's heart when his wife walks down Michigan Avenue and the shopkeepers know her by first name. We stayed in the same room at the Ritz Carlton each time we went – and we learned to love Chicago! We built new friendships and learned new skills.

In the fall of 1999 our lives were changed forever when Dr. Fred Aurbach told us about JuicePLUS+®. He walked up to me at Baylor College of Dentistry, where Frank was being honored as the past president of the Baylor Dental Alumni Association, and Dr. Aurbach was also being honored for having served in the same position, and he just asked me, "Have you ever heard of JuicePLUS+®?"

"No," I replied. "What is it?"

"It's seventeen different fresh raw fruits, vegetables, and grains in a capsule. Would you listen to a tape if it might improve your health?"

I was excited. I went over to Frank, and he rolled his eyes, and said, "Sara, do you have any idea how much of that junk I get across my desk every day? It's probably snake oil."

"But he's a colleague of yours."

"But didn't you notice?" Frank replied, "He talked to you, not to me."

Well, Frank was conducting a dental meeting at the Intercontinental at Dallas – Fort Worth Airport that weekend, and I was driving up to north Texas, another two hundred fifty miles, to watch my parents sit in their rocking chairs and rock, while we talked. So I just popped that little tape into my car's tape player, thinking: *It can't hurt if I just listen. He won't care if I just listen. Even if it is just snake oil.* As I listened to Dr. Richard Dubois' talk, "The Whole Truth in 15 Minutes" I thought: *This just makes sense. And it doesn't cost that much. It can't possibly hurt me. What if it helps?*

So I was loaded for bear when I picked Frank up at that airport hotel. I asked him if I could take it. "Yes," he said, "as long as you don't tell anybody." So I became a secret JuicePLUS+® taker, and the rest is history. When I went to the ophthalmic surgeon that year, she noticed positive tissue changes in my eyes. And by June of that year, I was off all arthritis medications, so some phenomenal changes were taking place, with the only explanation being the enhanced nutrition I was receiving by taking this concentrated whole food product. Our lives were changed forever as a result of our using and then distributing this remarkable product.

On April 10, 2002, our precious third grandchild, Rebekah, was born. I got to watch her birth. It was an earth-shattering experience for me. I am so afraid of hospitals and blood, but it was worth it all. As I write this, she's eight years old. She likes to play soccer and basketball. In fact, she is the only girl in the all-boy soccer league in College Station, Texas. She likes to travel; we went to Disney World together in the fall of 2010. Last Christmas, we went skiing together in Crested Butte, Colorado, where Frank taught her how to ski.

After I started using JuicePLUS+®, and had experienced such a positive effect on my own health, I started sharing what I'd found with Frank's patients and staff, and discovered that many of them wanted to know more about it. It was as if, when I shared the idea with them, a light bulb went on in their heads – "aha!"

Frank's "aha moment" came late one night when he was pondering the ethics of recommending a whole food supplement to patients. Like a light had gone on in his head, he realized that with the research that had already been done (and now there is so much more great gold standard research) he could not refrain from telling his patients about something that might help them.

At that time, and even today, doctors recommend a multivitamin to most patients, even though the best research into the research (called a meta-analysis) has shown that while multivitamins may not hurt you, they will not help you much, either. Now Frank and his other healthcare professional colleagues had something substantial and natural to recommend, so he just started doing that. No pressure, just information. Informed patients make better choices. Those who chose to take JuicePLUS+® had better results. It was as simple as that.

I became a National Marketing Director with Juice-PLUS+® in two years and seven months, with Frank becoming a National Marketing Director two years later. Since about 2005, we've been traveling and speaking for the company that makes the product. We don't get paid to endorse the product or to speak; we do it because we know people need it.

In about 2000, I had asked Frank, "If I can make as much money with JuicePLUS+® as you make in your dental practice, would you sell the practice?" Of course he laughed, and quickly agreed. Well, by 2007, I cashed in the promise. He sold his practice, and now we're together all the time, and loving it.

In 2008, we were able to give the twins a cruise – their choice. Josh chose Alaska, and Elizabeth chose the British Isles. Rebekah will get her turn very shortly. We had a wonderful time on the trips, except that Elizabeth got lost in Inverness, Scotland (home of the Loch Ness monster). I had told her to meet us at the castle in fifteen minutes, but when the bus was getting ready to go back to the ship, she was nowhere to be found. I went to the administrator of the castle and said, "I don't have a lot of money, but whatever I have, you can have – just find her. Call out the cops, the helicopters, the Queen – whatever you have to do. Just find her, please." Well, she had jogged into Inverness and then turned the wrong way and had gotten lost. That's all. Everything worked out okay. Josh caught a king salmon as the highlight of his trip. We have lots of pictures and many wonderful memories.

We love traveling. In 2010, we took a trip to Prague, and were there three days. Then we got on a river cruise and went from Budapest to Amsterdam, stopping at the University of Würzburg, where Frank talked with the head researcher on the study into the effect of JuicePLUS+® on periodontal health.

Sara Eggleston

When you reach the National Marketing Director level (the highest level) with JuicePLUS+® you get to make a five- minute speech at one of the two national meetings that year. When it was my turn, I said that I wanted Frank to go up there with me, which was not done in those days. But that's what we decided to do, so when Frank tried to come up on stage with me, our very good friend and colleague Sue Burdick tried to stop him, without much success, you might imagine, since she was dealing with two pretty strong-willed people. Besides, Frank was about two feet taller than she was. Later that night at an award dinner we both attended, Sue and I happened to be in the restroom at the same time. "Sara," she said, "I'm so embarrassed. I'm so embarrassed. I'm mortified. I did not know you were married to Dentist of the World. I'm so embarrassed."

We just laughed. Had Daddy heard that, he would have slapped his thigh, too. But then, he did hear that, didn't he?

Looking back, and looking ahead, I'm thankful for so much – for parents who loved me and gave me a solid foundation of faith and common sense, for brothers who have supported me in various ways all along the path, for a daughter who brought life and light into the darkness of those days (and still does now), for grandchildren who can carry the torch into the future, and for a wonderful husband who is not only the dentist of the world but a trustworthy follower of Jesus.

Most of all, I'm thankful for Jesus and His Father, God, who have carried me, as on eagles' wings all these years, through darkness and light, fear and even despair, to victory in His name. As it says in Exodus about Israel having been transported from bondage to freedom by the Lord God Almighty, so it applies to me: "I carried you on eagles' wings and brought you to myself" (Exodus 19:4, NIV).

Sara Eggleston

Appendix:
Lessons Learned
On The Journey

Part I

Living The Simple Life

Chapter 1: Just an Ordinary Farm Girl

1. Keep confidences when you are expected to do so.

2. Avoid hurting the feelings of others, especially when they might be embarrassed about something that has happened.

3. Be willing to say you're sorry when you've made a mistake.

4. Take care with the feelings of an adolescent – even if you think you're making fun of him/her rather innocently.

5. Realize that you can't work your way to heaven by trying to be good, because there is only One who is truly good and can give you His goodness through faith.

6. Seek to overcome irrational fears, whether of bugs or anything else, so your childhood phobias do not immobilize you as an adult.

Chapter 2: Frugality, Fun, and Frito Lay

1. Be willing to work hard and long hours . . . whatever it takes to get a job done.

2. When your children do things or threaten to do things, don't overreact, and they may decide there's a better way.

3. Never throw anything away that you or anybody else might be able to use.

4. Be willing to laugh at yourself – too many folks take themselves way too seriously.

5. Take care never to falsely accuse your children, for they may decide to do what they've been accused of, even if they might not do such things otherwise.

Part II

Living In Fear

Chapter 3: Blind Love, Bounced Checks, and Bad Company

1. If you fall blindly into love, solicit advice from those you trust.

2. If or when you are afraid, fall back upon the truths you have learned in the past.

3. When someone entrusted with your care suggests an alternative treatment, give it the benefit of the doubt. They could be right.

4. If certain very difficult things seem to repeat themselves, ask yourself what God may be trying to teach you through these cycles.

5. In really hard times, if you feel like God has abandoned you, cling to the hope that He is still there and He understands and cares.

6. Be willing to forgive others; otherwise, you may become a prisoner of the pain they've caused.

7. Accept the things you cannot change, change the things you can, and pray for the wisdom to know the difference.

Chapter 4: A Reign of Terror

1. Write this prayer on the "doorposts" of your heart: "I will ... to will ... the will of God."

2. Be thankful for those who laid a foundation for your faith when you were growing up.

3. If you feel down and hopeless and restless most of the time, seek medical help since these feelings may be signs of depression that can lead to despair.

4. Memorize Scripture passages related to hope and courage and faith, and cling to them when the going gets rough.

5. Acknowledge by faith that your future is really in the Lord's hands, and not your own.

6. If you are experiencing such guilt and pain that you feel "dirty" even when you've not done anything wrong, yourself, cast those cares upon the One who died for your sins and can heal the pain, take away your sense of guilt, and give you rest.

7. When you know the thing you should do, but you lack the emotions that might usually fuel the action in question, do the right thing and the emotions will follow.

Part III

Living By Faith

Chapter 5: A Bold Spirit

1. Be willing to pray a prayer of relinquishment – "Not my will, but Thine be done."

2. Take care about discussing politics with family members or close friends who may differ.

3. Enjoy humorous things when they happen, and replay them often. You might even try slapping your leg like my Daddy did when he laughed.

4. In terms of your perceptions, remember that "you see what you know." Realize that you have to know something – both intellectually and experientially – before you can effectively teach it to someone else.

5. If someone with authority (like the FBI) offends you, try to turn it around into something you can laugh about together.

6. Out of respect for others' time, strive to be as punctual as possible … while not forgetting that you can't start the first grade play when the heroine is crying because she cannot find her hat.

Chapter 6: Keepsakes, Copiers, and the Teaching Moment

1. Don't try to engage in sex education with your children unless they are ready to do so.

2. When you're a guest at an event, do not engage in critique of anyone or anything, unless you are absolutely sure that your listeners totally agree with your perspective.

3. If you have an opportunity to praise someone in a public setting, praise everyone who is there.

4. Use teachable moments to engage both children and parents in learning important lessons.

5. When the copier has a speck on its platen that you can't get off, take solace in the fact that life is pretty much like that most of the time, imperfect in some way.

Part IV

Living In Victory

Chapter 7: Married to the Dentist of the World – Serving the Creator of the World

1. Always remember that God is in charge, and that you can trust Him.

2. Share your successes with those who helped you achieve them, and acknowledge those people when you are recognized for what you've achieved.

3. Find creative ways to allow others to enjoy what you're enjoying, for example through the use of technology, even when they may be a great distance from you at that moment.

4. When someone has accidentally injured you, realize that what's done is done, and try to keep a calm demeanor.

5. Since leaders are made, not born, strive to develop your leadership skills so you can multiply your impact by passing on your knowledge, beliefs, and commitments to others.

6. When someone is really embarrassed about something they've done to you or said to you, laugh with them, not at them.

7. Remember that what has happened to you is not as important as how you take it, and what you make of it.

Sara Eggleston

HEALTHY LIFE PRESS

HELPING YOU TOWARD OPTIMAL HEALTH

WWW.HEALTHYLIFEPRESS.COM

CATALOG 2012.1 – December 2012

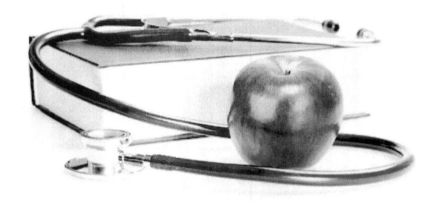

AN INDEPENDENT SMALL CHRISTIAN PUBLISHER WITH A BIG MISSION – TO HELP PEOPLE LIVE HEALTHIER LIVES PHYSICALLY, EMOTIONALLY, SPIRITUALLY, AND RELATIONALLY

HEALTHY LIFE PRESS
2603 Drake Drive
Orlando, FL 32810
Toll-free: 1-877-331-2766
E-mail: healthylifepress@aol.com

Resources from Healthy Life Press

We've Got Mail: The New Testament Letters in Modern English – As Relevant Today as Ever! by Rev. Warren C. Biebel, Jr. – A modern English paraphrase of the New Testament Letters, sure to inspire in readers a loving appreciation for God's Word. (Printed book: $9.95; PDF eBook: $6.95; together: $15.00; commercial eBook reader version: $9.99.)

Hearth & Home – Recipes for Life, by Karey Swan (7th Edition) – Far more than a cookbook, this classic is a life book, with recipes for life as well as for great food. Karey describes how to buy and prepare from scratch a wide variety of tantalizing dishes, while weaving into the book's fabric the wisdom of the ages plus the recipe that she and her husband used to raise their kids. A

great gift for Christmas or for a new bride. (Perfect Bound Version (8 x 10, glossy cover): $17.95; PDF eBook version: $12.95; Together as set: $24.95; commercial eBook reader version: $9.99.)

Who Me, Pray? Prayer 101: Praying Aloud, for Beginners, by Gary A. Burlingame – *Who Me, Pray?* is a practical guide for prayer, based on Jesus' direction in "The Lord's Prayer," with examples provided for use in typical situations where you might be asked or expected to pray in public. (Printed book: $6.95 PDF eBook: $2.99; together: $7.95.)

The Big Black Book – What the Christmas Tree Saw, by Rev. Warren C. Biebel, Jr – An original Christmas story, from the perspective of the Christmas tree. This little book is especially suitable for parents to read to their children at Christmas time or all year-round. (Printed book: $7.95; PDF eBook: $4.95; Together: $10.95; commercial eBook reader version: $6.95.)

My Broken Heart Sings, the poetry of Gary Burlingame – In 1987, Gary and his wife Debbie lost their son Christopher John, at only six months of age, to a chronic lung disease. This life-changing experience gave them a special heart for helping others through similar loss and pain. (Printed book: $10.95; PDF eBook: $6.95; Together: $13.95; commercial eBook reader version: $9.99.)

After Normal: One Teen's Journey Following Her Brother's Death, by Diane Aggen – Based on a journal the author kept following her younger brother's death. It offers helpful insights and understanding for teens facing a similar loss or for those who might wish to understand and help teens facing a similar loss. (Printed book: $11.95; PDF eBook: $6.95; together: $15.00; commercial eBook reader version: $8.99.)

In the Unlikely Event of a Water Landing – Lessons Learned from Landing in the Hudson River, by Andrew Jamison, MD. The author was flying standby on US Airways Flight 1549 toward Charlotte on January 15, 2009, from New York City, where he had been interviewing for a residency position. Little did he know that the next stop would be the Hudson River. Riveting and inspirational, this book would be especially helpful for people in need of hope and encouragement. (Printed book: $8.95; PDF eBook: $6.95; Together: $12.95; commercial eBook reader version: $8.99.)

Finding Martians in the Dark – Everything I Needed to Know About Teaching Took Me Only 30 Years to Learn, by Dan M. Biebel – Packed with wise advice based on hard experience, and laced with humor, this book is a perfect teacher's gift year-round. Susan J. Wegmann, PhD, says, "Biebel's sardonic wit is mellowed by a genuine love for kids and teaching. . . . A Whitman-like sensibility flows through his stories of teaching, learning, and life." (Printed book: $10.95; PDF eBook: $6.95; Together: $15.00; commercial eBook reader version: $9.99.)

Because We're Family and *Because We're Friends,* by Gary A. Burlingame – Sometimes things related to faith can be hard to discuss with your family and friends. These booklets are designed to be given as gifts, to help you open the door to discussing spiritual matters with family members and friends who are open to such a conversation. (Printed book: $5.95 each; PDF  eBook: $4.95 each; together: $9.95 per pair [printed & eBook of the same title]; commercial eBook reader version: $5.95.)

The Transforming Power of Story: How Telling Your Story Brings Hope to Others and Healing to Yourself, by Elaine Leong Eng, MD, and David B. Biebel, DMin – This book demonstrates, through multiple true life stories, how sharing one's story, especially in a group setting, can bring hope to listeners and healing to the one who shares. Individuals facing difficulties will find this book greatly encouraging. (Printed book: $14.99; PDF eBook: $9.99; together: $19.99; commercial eBook reader version: $9.99.)

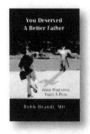

You Deserved a Better Father: Good Parenting Takes a Plan, by Robb Brandt, MD – About parenting by intention, and other lessons the author learned through the loss of his firstborn son. It is especially for parents who believe that bits and pieces of leftover time will be enough for their own children. (Printed book: $10.95 each; PDF eBook: $6.95; together: $12.95; commercial eBook reader version: $9.99.)

Jonathan, You Left Too Soon, by David B. Biebel, DMin – One pastor's journey through the loss of his son, into the darkness of depression, and back into the light of joy again, emerging with a renewed sense of mission. (Printed book: $6.00; PDF eBook: $5.99; together: $10.00.)

eBook Cover

Printed Cover

The Spiritual Fitness Checkup for the 50-Something Woman, by Sharon V. King, PhD – Following the stages of a routine medical exam, the author describes ten spiritual fitness "checkups" midlife women can conduct to assess their spiritual health and tone up their relationship with God. Each checkup consists of the author's personal reflections, a Scripture reference for meditation, and a "Spiritual Pulse Check," with exercises readers can use for personal application. (Printed book: $8.95; PDF eBook: $6.95; together: $12.95.)

Unless otherwise noted on the site itself, shipping is free in the continental USA for all products purchased through www.healthylifepress.com.

The Other Side of Life – Over 60? God Still Has a Plan for You, by Rev. Warren C. Biebel Jr. – Drawing on biblical examples and his 60-plus years of pastoral experience, Rev. Biebel helps older (and younger) adults understand God's view of aging and the rich life available to everyone who seeks a deeper relationship with God as they age. Rev. Biebel explains how to: Identify God's ongoing plan for your life; Rely on faith to manage the anxieties of aging; Form positive, supportive relationships; Cultivate patience; Cope with new technologies; Develop spiritual integrity; Understand the effects of dementia; Develop a Christ-centered perspective of aging. (Printed book: $10.95; PDF eBook: $6.95; together: $15.00; commercial eBook reader version: $9.99.)

My Faith, My Poetry by Gary A. Burlingame – This unique book of Christian poetry is actually two in one. The first collection of poems, *A Day in the Life*, explores a working parent's daily journey of faith. The reader is carried from morning to bedtime, from "In the Details," to "I Forgot to Pray," back to "Home Base," and finally to "Eternal Love Divine." The

second collection of poems, *Come Running*, is wonder, joy, and faith wrapped up in words that encourage and inspire the mind and the heart. (Printed book: $10.95; PDF eBook: $6.95; together: $13.95; commercial eBook reader version: $9.99.)

On Eagles' Wings, by Sara Eggleston – One woman's life journey from idyllic through chaotic to joy, carried all the way by the One who has promised to never leave us nor forsake us. Remarkable, poignant, moving, and inspiring, this autobiographical account will help many who are facing difficulties that seem too great to overcome or even bear at all. It is proof that Isaiah 40:31 is as true today as when it was penned, "But they that wait upon the LORD shall renew their strength; they shall mount up with wings as eagles; they shall run, and not be weary; and they shall walk, and not faint." (Printed book: $14.95; PDF eBook: $8.95; together: $22.95; commercial eBook reader version: $9.99.)

Richer Descriptions, by Gary A. Burlingame – A unique and handy manual, covering all <u>nine</u> human senses in seven chapters, for Christian speakers and writers. Exercises and a speaker's checklist equip speakers to engage their audiences in a richer experience. Writing examples and a writer's guide help writers bring more life to the characters and scenes of their stories. Bible references encourage a deeper appreciation of being created by God for a sensory existence. (Printed book: $15.95; PDF eBook: $8.95; together: $22.95; commercial eBook reader version: $9.99.)

Treasuring Grace, by Rob Plumley and Tracy Roberts – *This novel was inspired by a dream.* Liz Swanson's life isn't quite what she'd imagined, but she considers herself lucky. She has a good husband, beautiful children, and fulfillment outside of her home through volunteer work. On some days she doesn't even notice the dull ache in her heart. While she's preparing for their summer kickoff at Lake George, the ache disappears and her sudden happiness is mistaken for anticipation of their weekend. However, as the family heads north, there are clouds on the horizon that have nothing to do with the weather. Only Liz's daughter, who's found some of her mother's hidden journals, has any idea what's wrong. But by the end of the weekend, there will be no escaping the truth or its painful buried secrets. Printed: $12.95; PDF eBook: $7.95; together: $19.95; commercial eBook reader version: $9.99.

Life's A Symphony, by Mary Z. Smith – When Kate Spence Cooper receives the news that her husband, Jack, has been killed in the war, she and her young son Jeremy move back to Crawford Wood, Tennessee to be closer to family. Since Jack's death Kate feels that she's lost trust in everyone, including God. Will she ever find her way back to the only One whom she can always depend upon? And what about Kate's match making brother, Chance? The cheeky man has other ideas on how to bring happiness into his sister's life once more. (Printed book: $12.95; PDF eBook: $7.95; together: $19.95; commercial eBook reader version: $9.99.)

Your Mind at Its Best – 40 Ways To Keep Your Brain Sharp by David B. Biebel, DMin; James E. Dill, MD; and, Bobbie Dill, RN – Everyone wants their mind to function at high levels throughout life. In 40 easy-to-understand chapters, readers will discover a wide variety of tips and tricks to keep their minds sharp. Synthesizing science and self-help, *Your Mind at Its Best* makes fascinating  neurological discoveries understandable and immediately applicable to readers of any age. (Printed book: $13.99.)

From Orphan to Physician – The Winding Path, by Chun-Wai Chan, MD – From the foreword: "In this book, Dr. Chan describes how his family escaped to Hong Kong, how they survived in utter poverty, and how he went from being an orphan to graduating from Harvard Medical School and becoming a cardiologist. The writing is fluent, easy to read and understand. The sequence of events is realistic, emotionally moving, spiritually touching, heart-warming, and thought provoking. The book illustrates . . . how one must have faith in order to walk through life's winding path." (Printed book: $14.95; PDF eBook: $8.95; together: $22.95; commercial eBook reader version: $9.99.)

12 Parables, by Wayne Faust – Timeless Christian stories about doubt, fear, change, grief, and more. Using tight, entertaining prose, professional musician and comedy performer Wayne Faust manages to deal with difficult concepts in a simple, straightforward way. These are stories you can read aloud over and over—to your spouse, your family, or in a group setting. Packed with emotion and just enough mystery to keep you wondering, while providing lots of points to ponder and discuss when you're through, these stories relate the gospel in the tradition of the greatest speaker of parables the world has ever known, who appears in them often. (Printed book: $14.95; PDF eBook: $8.95; together: $22.95; commercial eBook reader version: $9.99.)

The Answer is Always "Jesus," by Aram Haroutunian, who gave children's sermons for 15 years at a large church in Golden, Colorado—well over 500 in all. This book contains 74 of his most unforgettable presentations—due to the children's responses. Pastors, home-schoolers, parents who often lead family devotions, or other storytellers will find these stories, along with comments about props and how to prepare and present them, an invaluable asset in reconnecting with the simplest, most profound truths of Scripture, and then to envision how best to communicate these so even a child can understand them.(Printed book: $12.95; PDF eBook: $8.95; together: $19.95; commercial eBook reader version: $9.99.)

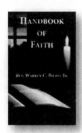

Handbook of Faith by Rev. Warren C. Biebel Jr. – The *New York Times World 2011 Almanac* claimed that there are 2 billion, 200 thousand Christians in the world, with "Christians" being defined as "followers of Christ." The original 12 followers of Christ changed the world; indeed, they changed the history of the world. So this author, a pastor with over 60 years' experience, poses and answers this logical question: "If there are so many 'Christians' on this planet, why are they so relatively ineffective in serving the One they claim to follow?" Answer: Because, unlike Him, they do not know and trust the Scriptures, implicitly. This little volume will help you do that. (Printed book: $8.95; PDF eBook: $6.95; together: $13.95; commercial eBook reader version: $8.95.)

Pieces of My Heart, by David L. Wood – Eighty-two lessons from normal everyday life. David's hope is that these stories will spark thoughts about God's constant involvement and intervention in our lives and stir a sense of how much He cares about every detail that is important to us. The piece missing represents his son, Daniel, who died in a fire shortly before his first birthday. (Printed book: $16.95; PDF eBook: $8.95; Set: $24.95; commercial eBook reader version: $9.99.)

!!!!!*UPDATE*!!!!! *Pieces of My Heart* is also available in two volumes. Vol. 1 is the first 39 chapters of this inspiring book; Vol. 2 is chapters 40-82 of the larger volume. (Each of these new volumes are $10.95 for the printed book, $6.95 for the PDF eBook version; $14.95 for the set; commercial eBook reader version: $8.95.)

Couples have enjoyed reading these two volumes concurrently, then discussing the great lessons they contain.

Dream House by Justa Carpenter – Written by a New England builder of several hundred homes, the idea for this book came to him one day as he was driving that came to him one day as was driving from one job site to another. He pulled over and recorded it so he would remember it, and now you will remember it, too, if you believe, as he does, that ". . . He who has begun a good work in you will complete it until the day of Jesus Christ." (Printed book: $8.95; PDF eBook: $6.95; Set: $13.95; commercial eBook reader version: $8.95.)

A Simply Homemade Clean, by homesteader Lisa Barthuly – "Somewhere along the path, it seems we've lost our gumption, the desire to make things ourselves," says the author. "Gone are the days of 'do it yourself.' Really . . . why bother? There are a slew of retailers just waiting for us with anything and everything we could need; packaged up all pretty, with no thought  or effort required. It is the manifestation of 'progress' . . . right?" I don't buy that!" Instead, Lisa describes how to make safe and effective cleansers for home, laundry, and body right in your own home. This saves money and avoids exposure to harmful chemicals often found in commercially produced cleansers. (Printed book: $10.95; PDF eBook: $6.95; Set: $14.95; commercial eBook reader version: $8.95.)

ABOUT HEALTHY LIFE PRESS

Healthy Life Press was founded with a primary goal of helping previously unpublished authors to get their works to market, and to reissue worthy, previously published works that were no longer available. Our mission is to help people toward optimal vitality by providing resources promoting physical, emotional, spiritual, and relational health as viewed from a Christian perspective. We see health as a verb, and achieving optimal health as a process—a crucial process for followers of Christ if we are to love the Lord with all our heart, soul, mind, AND strength, and our neighbors as ourselves—for as long as He leaves us here. We are a collaborative and cooperative small Christian publisher.

For information about publishing with us,
e-mail: healthylifepress@aol.com.

RECOMMENDED RESOURCES – PRO-LIFE DVD SERIES

SEE WWW.HEALTHYLIFEPRESS.COM (SELECT "DVD") FOR TRAILERS AND SPECIAL COMBINATION PRICING

EYEWITNESS 2 (PUBLIC SCHOOL VERSION) – This DVD has been used in many public schools. It is a fascinating journey through 38 weeks of pregnancy, showing developing babies via cutting edge digital ultrasound technology. Separate chapters allow viewing distinct segments individually. (List Price: $34.95; Sale Price: $24.95.)

WINDOW TO THE WOMB (2 DVD DISC SET) Disc 1: Ian Donald (1910-1987) "A Prophetic Legacy;" Disc 2: "A Journey from Death To Life" (50 min) – Includes history of sonography and its increasing impact against abortion—more than 80% of expectant parents who "see" their developing baby choose for life. Perfect for counseling and education in Pregnancy Centers, Christian schools, homeschools, and churches. (List: $49.95; Sale: $34.95.)

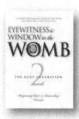

WINDOW TO THE WOMB (PREGNANCY CARE & COUNSELING VERSION) – Facts about fetal development, abortion complications, post-abortion syndrome, and healing. Separate chapters allow selection of specialized presentations to accommodate the needs and time constraints of their situations. (List: $34.95; Sale: $24.95.)

Unless otherwise noted on the site itself, shipping is free in the continental USA for all products purchased through www.healthylifepress.com.

RECOMMENDED RESOURCES – BOOKS

If God Is So Good, Why Do I Hurt So Bad?, by David B. Biebel, DMin – In this best-selling classic (over 200,000 copies in print worldwide, in five languages) on the subject of loss and renewal, first published in 1989, the author comes alongside people in pain, and shows the way through and beyond it, to joy again. This book has proven helpful to those who are struggling and to those who wish to understand and help. Revised and re-released July 2010. (Printed book: $12.95; PDF eBook: $8.95; Set: $19.95.)

52 Ways to Feel Great Today, by David B. Biebel, DMin, James E. Dill, MD, and Bobbie Dill, RN – **Increase Your Vitality, Improve your Outlook.** Simple, fun, inexpensive things you can do to increase your vitality and improve your outlook. Why live an "ordinary" life when you could be experiencing the extraordinary? Don't settle for good enough when "great" is such a short stretch away. Make today great! (Printed book: $14.99.)

The A to Z Guide To Healthier Living, by David B. Biebel, DMin, James E. Dill, MD, and Bobbie Dill, RN – You'll find great info on: avoiding fad diets, being kind to your GI tract, building healthy bones, finding contentment, getting a good night's sleep, keeping your relationships strong, simplifying your life, staying creative, and much more. (Printed book: 12.99; commercial eBook reader versions: $8.99.)

New Light on Depression, a CBA Gold Medallion winner, by David B. Biebel, DMin, and Harold Koenig, MD – The most exhaustive Christian resource on a subject that is more common than we might wish. Hope for those with depression and help for those who love them. (Printed book: $15.00.)

VOWS, a Romantic novel by F.F. Whitestone – When the police cruiser pulled up to the curb outside, Faith Framingham's heart skipped a beat, for she could see that Chuck, who should have been driving, was not in the vehicle. Chuck's partner, Sandy, stepped out slowly. Sandy's pursed lips and ashen face spoke volumes. Faith waited by the front door, her hands clasped tightly, to counter the fact that her mind was already reeling. "Love never fails." A compelling story. (Printed book: $12.99; full color PDF eBook: $9.99. Combination, only from publisher: $19.99. Other eReader options: BN.com and Amazon.com.)

Our God Given Senses, by Gary A. Burlingame – Did you know humans have NINE senses? The Bible draws on these senses to reveal spiritual truth. We are to taste and see that the Lord is a good. We are to carry the fragrance of Christ. Our faith is produced upon hearing. Jesus asked Thomas to touch him. God created us for a sensory experience and that is what you will find in

this book. (Printed book: $12.99; full color PDF eBook: $9.99; together: $19.99, direct from publisher; other eReader options: BN.com and Amazon.com. Available Spring 2013.)

God Loves You Circle, by Michelle Johnson – Daily inspiration for your deeper walk with Christ. This collection of short stories of Christian living will make you laugh, make you cry, but most of all make you contemplate–the meaning and value of walking with the Master moment-by-moment, day-by-day. (Printed book: $17.95; full color PDF eBook: $9.99; together $24.95, direct from publisher; commercial eBook reader versions: $9.99; full color, signed book: $29.99 [late 2012].)

Unless otherwise noted on the site itself, shipping is free in the continental USA for all products purchased through www.healthylifepress.com.